MAHATMA GANDHI
ON HINDUISM

MAHATMA GANDHI
ON HINDUISM

Published by
Rupa Publications India Pvt. Ltd 2022
7/16, Ansari Road, Daryaganj
New Delhi 110002

Sales centres:
Allahabad Bengaluru Chennai
Hyderabad Jaipur Kathmandu
Kolkata Mumbai

Edition Copyright © Rupa Publications India Pvt. Ltd 2022

All rights reserved.
No part of this publication may be reproduced, transmitted,
or stored in a retrieval system, in any form or by any means,
electronic, mechanical, photocopying, recording or otherwise,
without the prior permission of the publisher.

ISBN: 978-93-5520-772-2

First impression 2022

10 9 8 7 6 5 4 3 2 1

Printed in India

This book is sold subject to the condition that it shall not,
by way of trade or otherwise, be lent, resold, hired out, or otherwise
circulated, without the publisher's prior consent, in any form of
binding or cover other than that in which it is published.

To the Students of Life

Character cannot be built with mortar and stone. It cannot be built by hands other than your own. The Principal and the Professor cannot give you character from the pages of books. Character building comes from their very lives and really speaking, it must come from within yourselves.

Put all your knowledge, learning and scholarship in one scale and truth and purity in the other and the latter will by far outweigh the other.

—Mohandas Karamchand (M.K.) Gandhi,
The Selected Works of Mahatma Gandhi: The Voice of Truth,
Vol. 6, Navajivan Publishing House, 1968.

Contents

RELIGION

1.	On the Omnipresence of Religion	3
2.	Fundamentals of Hinduism	12
3.	Facets of Hinduism	15
4.	Why I Am a Hindu	19
5.	Sanatani Hindu	22
6.	My Understanding of Hinduism	26
7.	Fasting in Satyagraha	29
8.	Between Violence and Cowardice	31
9.	Cow Worship in Hinduism	36
10.	Cow Protection	40
11.	Brahmacharya: The Virtue of Chastity	45
12.	Hindu Code of Conduct	50
13.	Contemporary Hinduism	55
14.	Misinterpretation of Hinduism	60
15.	Beyond Religious Boundaries	63
16.	Hinduism's Contribution to the Civilization	66
17.	The Law of Varna	70
18.	Shortcomings of Hinduism	72
19.	On Women's Status	77
20.	My Views on Untouchability	83
21.	My Case against Untouchability	86
22.	Defending Tulsidas's Ramayana	89
23.	Satan in Hinduism	93
24.	The Ethical Religion of Higher Morality	96

25. The Hindu–Muslim Feud	99
26. Die without Killing	101
27. Himsa in the Gita	104
28. The Gita in My Understanding	113
29. The Gita from Yeravda	122
30. The Philosophy of Non-Violence	125
31. On Change of Faith	127
32. The Way to Peace	131

FAITH

33. The Analogy of Faith	141
34. My Faith in God	143
35. My Belief in an Indefinable Power	147
36. The Voice of God	151
37. Many Yet One: My Experience with God	154
38. Advaitism and God	158
39. On Idol Worship	161
40. Approach Temples in Faith	165
41. The Spinning Wheel and God	167
42. Krishna in the Gita of Karma	172
43. Ramanama	175
44. Ramadhun	177
45. The Remedy of Ramanama	179
46. Ramarajya	181

TRUTH

47. What Is Truth?	187
48. The Ultimate Truth	191
49. The Power of Truth	194
50. Truth and Love	196
51. Truth and Beauty	200
52. My Mission	205

Religion

Religion

1

On the Omnipresence of Religion

Religion should pervade every one of our actions. Here religion does not mean sectarianism. It means a belief in ordered moral government of the universe. It is not less real because it is unseen. This religion transcends Hinduism, Islam, Christianity, etc. It does not supersede them. It harmonizes them and gives them reality.

—Gandhi, M.K., *Harijan*, 10 February 1940, p. 445.

No man can live without religion. There are some who in the egotism of their reason declare that they have nothing to do with religion. But it is like a man saying that he breathes but that he has no nose. Whether by reason, or by instinct, or by superstition, man acknowledges some sort of relationship with the divine. The rankest agnostic or atheist does acknowledge the need of a moral principle, and associates something good with its observance and something bad with its non-observance. Bradlaugh, whose atheism is well-known, always insisted on proclaiming his innermost conviction. He had to suffer a lot for thus speaking the truth, but he delighted in it and said that truth is its own reward. Not that he was quite insensible to the joy resulting from the observance of truth. This joy however is not at all worldly, but springs out of communion with the divine. That is why I have said that even a man who disowns religion cannot and does not live without religion.

—Gandhi, M.K., *Young India*, 23 January 1930, p. 25.

I reject any religious doctrine that does not appeal to reason and is in conflict with morality. I tolerate unreasonable religious sentiment when it is not immoral.

—Gandhi, M.K., *Young India*, 21 July 1920, p. 4.

As soon as we lose the moral basis, we cease to be religious. There is no such thing as religion overriding morality. Man, for instance, cannot be untruthful, cruel and incontinent and claim to have God on his side.

—Gandhi, M.K., *Young India*, 24 November 1921, p. 385.

Religion which takes no account of practical affairs and does not help to solve them, is no religion.

—Gandhi, M.K., *Young India*, 7 May 1925, p. 164.

Every activity of a man of religion must be derived from his religion, because religion means being bound to God, that is to say, God rules your every breath.

—Gandhi, M.K., *Harijan*, 2 March 1934, p. 23.

From my sixth or seventh year up to my sixteenth I was at school, being taught all sorts of things except religion. I may say that I failed to get from the teachers what they could have given me without any effort on their part. And yet I kept on picking up things here and there from my surroundings. The term 'religion' I am using in its broadest sense, meaning thereby self-realization or knowledge of self.

Being born in the Vaishnava faith, I had often to go to the *Haveli*. But it never appealed to me. I did not like its glitter and pomp. Also I heard rumours of immorality being practised there, and lost all interest in it. Hence I could gain nothing from the *Haveli*.

But what I failed to get there I obtained from my nurse, an old servant of the family, whose affection for me I still recall. I have said before that there was in me a fear of ghosts and spirits. Rambha, for that was her name, suggested, as a remedy for this fear, the repetition of Ramanama. I had more faith in her than in her remedy, and so at a tender age I began repeating Ramanama to cure my fear of ghosts and spirits. This was of course short-lived, but the good seed sown in childhood was not sown in vain. I think it is due to the seed sown by that good woman Rambha that today Ramanama is an infallible remedy for me.

What, however, left a deep impression on me was the reading of the Ramayana before my father. During part of his illness my father was in Porbandar. There every evening he used to listen to the Ramayana. The reader was a great devotee of Rama. He had a melodious voice. He would sing the *Dohas* (couplets) and *Chopais* (quatrains), and explain them, losing himself in the discourse and carrying his listeners along with him. I must have been thirteen at that time, but I quite remember being enraptured by his reading. That laid the foundation of my deep devotion to the Ramayana. Today I regard the Ramayana of Tulsidas as the greatest book in ail devotional literature.

A few months after this we came to Rajkot. There was no Ramayana reading there. The Bhagavat, however, used to be read on every *Ekadashi* day. Sometimes, I attended the reading, but the reciter was uninspiring. Today I see that the Bhagavat is a book which can evoke religious fervour. I have read it in Gujarati with intense interest. But when I heard portions of the original read by Pandit Madan Mohan Malaviya during my twenty-one days' fast. I wished I had heard it in my childhood from such a devotee as he is, so that I could have formed a liking for it at an early age. Impressions formed at that age strike roots deep down into one's nature, and it is my perpetual regret that I was not fortunate enough to hear more good books of this kind read during that period.

In Rajkot, however, I got an early grounding in toleration for all branches of Hinduism and sister religions. For my father and mother would visit the *Haveli* as also Shiva's and Rama's temples and would take or send us youngsters there. Jain monks also would pay frequent visits to my father, and would even go out of their way to accept food from us—non-Jains. They would have talks with my father on subjects religious and mundane.

He had, besides, Mussalman and Parsi friends, who would talk to him about their own faiths, and he would listen to them always with respect, and often with interest. Being his nurse, I often had a chance to be present at these talks. These many things combined to inculcate in me a toleration for all faiths. Only Christianity was at the time an exception. I developed a sort of dislike for it. And for a reason. In those days Christian missionaries used to stand in a corner near the high school and hold forth, pouring abuse on Hindus and their gods. I could not endure this. I must have stood there to hear them once only, but that was enough to dissuade me from repeating the experiment. About the same time, I heard of a well-known Hindu having been converted to Christianity.

It was the talk of the town that, when he was baptized he had to eat beef and drink liquor, that he also had to change his clothes, and that thenceforth he began to go about in European costume including a hat. These things got on my nerves. Surely, thought I, a religion that compelled one to eat beef, drink liquor, and change one's own clothes did not deserve the name. I also heard that the new convert had already begun abusing the religion of his ancestors, their customs and their country. All these things created in me a dislike for Christianity. But the fact that I had learnt to be tolerant to other religions did not mean that I had any living faith in God.

But one thing took deep root in me—the conviction that morality is the basis of things, and that truth is the substance of all morality. Truth became my sole objective. It began to grow in magnitude every day and my definition of it also has been ever widening.

A Gujarati didactic stanza likewise gripped my mind and heart. Its precept—return good for evil—became my guiding principle. It became such a passion with me that I began numerous experiments in it. Here are those (for me) wonderful lines:

> For a bowl of water give a goodly meal;
> For a kindly greeting bow thou down with zeal;
> For a simple penny pay thou back with gold;
> If thy life be rescued, life do not withhold.

> Thus the words and actions of the wise regard;
> Every little service tenfold they reward.
> But the truly noble know all men as one,
> And return with gladness good for evil done.

—Gandhi, M.K., *The Story of My Experiments with Truth*, Mahadev Desai (trans.), Navajivan Publishing House, 1948, pp. 12–13.

My father was a lover of his clan, truthful, brave and generous, but short-tempered. Of religious training he had very little, but he had that kind of religious culture which frequent visits to temples and listening to religious discourses make available to many Hindus. In his last days he began reading the *Gita* at the instance of a learned Brahmana friend of the family, and he used to repeat aloud some verses every day at the time of worship.

The outstanding impression my mother has left on my memory is that of saintliness. She was deeply religious. She would not think of taking her meals without her daily prayers. Going to *Haveli*—the Vaishnava temple—was one of her daily duties. As far as my memory can go back, I do not remember her having ever missed the *Chaturmas*. She would take the hardest vows and keep them without flinching. Illness was no excuse for relaxing them. I can recall her once falling ill when she was observing the *Chandrayana* vow, but the illness was not allowed to interrupt the observance. To keep two or three consecutive fasts was nothing to her. Living on one meal a day during *Chaturmas* was a habit with her. Not content with that she fasted every alternate day during one *Chaturmas*. During another *Chaturmas* she vowed not to have food without seeing the sun. We children on those days would stand, staring at the sky, waiting to announce the appearance of the sun to our mother. Everyone knows that at the height of the rainy season the sun often does not condescend to show his face. And I remember days when, at his sudden appearance, we would rush and announce it to her. She would run out to see with her own eyes, but by that time the fugitive sun would be gone, thus depriving her of her meal. "That does not matter," she would say cheerfully, "God did not want me to eat today." And then she would return to her round of duties.

—Gandhi, M.K., *The Story of My Experiments with Truth*, Mahadev Desai (trans.), Navajivan Publishing House, 1948, pp. 12–13.

Scientists tell us that without the presence of the cohesive force amongst the atoms that comprise this globe of ours, it would crumble to pieces and we would cease to exist; and even as there is cohesive force in blind matter, so must there be in all things animate, and the name for that cohesive force among animate beings is Love. We notice it between father and son, between brother and sister, friend and friend. But we have to learn to use that force among all that lives, and in the use of it consists our knowledge of God.

—Gandhi, M.K., *Young India*, 5 May 1920, p. 7.

I claim that even now, though the social structure is not based on a conscious acceptance of non-violence, all the world over mankind lives and men retain their possessions on the sufferance of one another. If they had not done so, only the fewest and the most ferocious would have survived. But such is not the case. Families are bound together by ties of love, and so are groups in the so-called civilized society called nations. Only they do not recognize the supremacy of the law of non-violence. It follows, therefore, that they have not investigated its vast possibilities. Hitherto out of sheer inertia, shall I say, we have taken it for granted that complete non-violence is possible only for the few who take the vow of non-possession and the allied abstinences. Whilst it is true that the votaries alone can carry on research work and declare from time to time the new possibilities of the great eternal law governing man, if it is the law, it must hold good for all. The many failures we see are not of the law but of the followers, many of whom do not even know that they are under that law willy-nilly. When a mother dies for her child she unknowingly obeys the law. I have been pleading for the past fifty years for a conscious acceptance of the law and its zealous practice even in the face of failures. Fifty years' work has shown marvellous results and strengthened my faith.

—Gandhi, M.K., *Harijan*, 22 February 1942, p. 48.

I have suggested in these columns that woman is the incarnation of Ahimsa. Ahimsa means infinite love, which again means infinite capacity for suffering. Who but woman, the mother of man, shows this capacity in the largest measure? She shows it as she carries the infant and feeds it during nine months and derives joy in the suffering involved. What can beat the suffering caused by the pangs of labour? But she forgets them in the joy of creation. Who again suffers daily so that her babe may wax from day to day ? Let her transfer that love to the whole of humanity, let her forget that she ever was or can be the object of man's lust. And she will occupy her proud position by the side of man as his mother, maker and silent leader. It is given to her to teach the art of peace to the warring world thirsting for that nectar.

—Gandhi, M.K., *Harijan*, 24 February 1940, p. 13.

2

Fundamentals of Hinduism

In the purest type of Hinduism a brahmana, an ant, an elephant and a dog-eater (*shwapacha*) are of the same status. And because our philosophy is so high, and we have failed to live up to it, that very philosophy today stinks in our nostrils. Hinduism insists on the brotherhood not only of all mankind but of all that lives. It is a conception which makes one giddy, but we have to work up to it. The moment we have restored real living equality between man and man, we shall be able to establish equality between man and the whole creation. When that day comes we shall have peace on earth and goodwill to men.

— Gandhi, M.K., 'A Talk with Rao Bhadur Rajah', *Harijan*, Vol. 4, No. 7, 28 March 1936, p. 51.

[T]he whole of Hinduism could be summed up in the first verse of the Ishopanishad...

ईशावास्यमिदं सर्वं यत्किञ्च जगत्यां जगत् ।
तेन त्यक्तेन भुञ्जीथा मा गृधः कस्य स्विद्धनम् ॥१॥

Those who know a little bit of Sanskrit will find that there is nothing abstruse there that you find in other Vedic *mantras*, and its meaning is simply this: All that there is in this Universe, great or small, including the tiniest atom, is pervaded by God, known as Creator or Lord... Thus, he says, renounce everything, i.e., everything that is on this Universe, the whole of the Universe, and not only this tiny globe of ours, renounce it...

—Gandhi, M.K., 'The Haripad Speech', *Harijan*, Vol. 4, No. 51, 30 January 1937, p. 407.

'Since God pervades everything, nothing belongs to you, not even your own body. God is the undisputed, unchallengeable Master of everything you possess.' And so when a person who calls himself a Hindu goes through the process of regeneration or a second birth, as Christians would call it, he has to perform a dedication or renunciation of all that he has in ignorance called his own property. And then when he has performed this act of dedication or renunciation, he is told that he will win a reward in the shape of God taking good care of what he will require for food, clothing or housing. Therefore, the condition of enjoyment or use of the necessaries of life is their dedication or renunciation. And that dedication or renunciation has got to be done from day to day, lest we may in this busy world forget the central fact of life. And to crown all, the seer says: 'Covet not anybody's riches.' I suggest to you that the truth that is embedded in this very short *mantra* is calculated to satisfy the highest cravings of every human being whether they have reference to this world or to the next. I have in my search of the scriptures of the world found nothing to add to this *mantra*. Looking back upon all the little I have read of the scriptures—it is precious little I confess—I feel that everything good in all the scriptures is derived from this *mantra*. If it is universal brotherhood—not only brotherhood of all human beings, but of all living beings—I find it in this *mantra*. If it is unshakable faith in the Lord and Master—and all the adjectives you can think of—I find it in this *mantra*. If it is the idea of complete surrender to God and of the faith that He will supply all that I need then again, I say I find it in this *mantra*. Since He pervades every fibre of my being and of all of you, I derive from it the doctrine of equality of all creatures on earth and it should satisfy the cravings of all philosophical communists. This *mantra* tells me that I cannot hold as mine anything that belongs to God, and if my life and that of all who believe in this *mantra* has to be a life of perfect dedication, it follows that it will have to be a life of continual service of our fellow creatures.

This, I say, is my faith and should be the faith of all who call themselves Hindus. And I venture to suggest to my Christian and Mussulman friends that they will find nothing more in their scriptures if they will search them[...] The very canons of interpretation laid down by Hinduism teach me that whatever is inconsistent with the truth I have expounded to you and which is hidden in the *mantra* I have named, must be summarily rejected as not belonging to Hinduism.

— Gandhi, M.K., 'The Kottayam Speech', *Harijan*, Vol. 4, No. 51, 30 January 1937, pp. 409–10.

3

Facets of Hinduism

[…] I have asserted my claim to being a Sanatani Hindu […] and yet there are things which are commonly done in the name of Hinduism, which I disregard. I have no desire to be called a Sanatani Hindu or any other if I am not such…

It is therefore necessary for me once and for all distinctly to give my meaning of Sanatana Hinduism. The word Sanatana I use in its natural sense.

I call myself a Sanatani Hindu, because,

1. I believe in the Vedas, the Upanishads, the Puranas and all that goes by the name of Hindu scriptures, and therefore in avatar as and rebirth,
2. I believe in the *Varnashrama dharma* in a sense, in my opinion, strictly Vedic but not in its present popular and crude sense,
3. I believe in the protection of the cow in its much larger sense than the popular,
4. I do not disbelieve in idol-worship.

The reader will note that I have purposely refrained from using the word divine origin in reference to the Vedas or any other scriptures. For I do not believe in the exclusive divinity of the Vedas. I believe the Bible, the Koran, and the

Zend Avesta to be as much divinely inspired as the Vedas. My belief in the Hindu scriptures does not require me to accept every word and every verse as divinely inspired. Nor do I claim to have any first-hand knowledge of these wonderful books. But I do claim to know and feel the truths of the essential teaching of the scriptures... I decline to be bound by any interpretation, however learned it may be, if it is repugnant to reason or moral sense. I do most emphatically repudiate the claim (if they advance any such) of the present Shankaracharyas and Shastris to give a correct interpretation of the Hindu scriptures. On the contrary I believe that our present knowledge of these books is in a most chaotic state. I believe implicitly in the Hindu aphorism, that no one truly knows the Shastras who has not attained perfection in Innocence (*Ahimsa*), Truth (*Satya*) and Self-Control (*Brahmacharya*) and who has not renounced all acquisition or possession of wealth. I believe in the institution of Gurus, but in this age millions must go without a Guru, because it is a rare thing to find a combination of perfect purity and perfect learning. But one need not despair of ever knowing the truth of one's religion, because the fundamentals of Hinduism, as of every great religion, are unchangeable, and easily understood.

—Gandhi, M.K., 'Hinduism', *Young India*, Vol. 3, No. 40, 6 October 1921, pp. 317–9.

Hinduism is a relentless pursuit after truth and if to-day it has become moribund, inactive, irresponsive to growth, it is because we are fatigued; and as soon as the fatigue is over, Hinduism will burst forth upon the world with a brilliance perhaps unknown before. Of course, therefore, Hinduism is the most tolerant of all religions. Its creed is all-embracing.

—Gandhi, M.K., 'What is Hinduism?', *Young India*, Vol. 6, No. 17, 24 April 1924, p. 136.

I can no more describe my feeling for Hinduism than for my own wife. She moves me as no other woman in the world can. Not that she has no faults. I dare say she has many more than I see myself. But the feeling of an indissoluble bond is there. Even so I feel for and about Hinduism with all its faults and limitations. Nothing elates me so much as the music of the Gita or the Ramayana by Tulsidas, the only two books in Hinduism I may be said to know. When I fancied I was taking my last breath the Gita was my solace. I know the vice that is going on to-day in all the great Hindu shrines, but I love them in spite of their unspeakable failings. There is an interest which I take in them and which I take in no other. I am a reformer through and through. But my zeal never takes me to the rejection of any of the essential things of Hinduism. I have said I do not disbelieve in idol-worship. An idol does not excite any feeling of veneration in me. But I think that idol-worship is part of human nature. We hanker after symbolism. Why should one be more composed in a church than elsewhere? Images are an aid to worship. No Hindu considers an image to be God. I do not consider idol-worship a sin.

It is clear from the foregoing, that Hinduism is not an exclusive religion. In it there is room for the worship of all the prophets of the world. It is not a missionary religion in the ordinary sense of the term. It has no doubt absorbed many tribes in its fold, but this absorption has been of an evolutionary imperceptible character. Hinduism tells everyone to worship God according to his own faith or *Dharma*, and so it lives at peace with all the religions... Hinduism is a growth of ages. In my opinion the beauty of Hinduism lies in its all-embracing inclusiveness. What the divine author of the Mahabharata said of his great creation is equally true of Hinduism. What of substance is contained in any other religion is always to be found in Hinduism. And what is not contained in it is insubstantial or unnecessary.

—Gandhi, M.K., 'Hinduism', *Young India*, Vol. 3, No. 40, 6 October 1921, pp. 317–19.

4

Why I Am a Hindu

An American friend who subscribes herself as a lifelong friend of India writes:

> As Hinduism is one of the prominent religions of the East, and as you have made a study of Christianity and Hinduism, and on the basis of that study have announced that you are a Hindu, I beg leave to ask of you if you will do me the favour to give me your reasons for that choice. Hindus and Christians alike realize that man's chief need is to know God and to worship Him in spirit and in truth. Believing that Christ was a revelation of God, Christians of America have sent to India thousands of their sons and daughters to tell the people of India about Christ. Will you in return kindly give us your interpretation of Hinduism and make a comparison of Hinduism with the teachings of Christ? I will be deeply grateful for this favour.

I have ventured at several missionary meetings to tell English and American missionaries that if they could have refrained from 'telling' India about Christ and had merely lived the life enjoined upon them by the Sermon on the Mount, India instead of suspecting them would have appreciated their living in the midst of her children and directly profited by their presence. Holding this view, I can 'tell' American friends nothing about Hinduism by way of 'return'. I do not believe in people telling others of their faith, especially with a view to conversion. Faith does not admit of telling. It has to be lived and then it becomes self-propagating.

Nor do I consider myself fit to interpret Hinduism except through my own life. And if I may not interpret Hinduism through my written word, I may not compare it with Christianity. The only thing it is possible for me therefore to do is to say as briefly as I can, why I am a Hindu.

Believing as I do in the influence of heredity, being born in a Hindu family, I have remained a Hindu. I should reject it, if I found it inconsistent with my moral sense or my spiritual growth. On examination I have found it to be the most tolerant of all religions known to me. Its freedom from dogma makes a forcible appeal to me inasmuch as it gives the votary the largest scope for self-expression. Not being an exclusive religion, it enables the followers of that faith not merely to respect all the other religions, but it also enables them to admire and assimilate whatever may be good in the other faiths. Non-violence is common to all religions, but it has found the highest expression and application in Hinduism. (I do not regard Jainism or Buddhism as separate from Hinduism.) Hinduism believes in the oneness not of merely all human life but in the oneness of all that lives. Its worship of the cow is, in my opinion, its unique contribution to the evolution of humanitarianism. It is a practical application of the belief in the oneness and, therefore, sacredness, of all life. The great belief in transmigration is a direct consequence of that belief. Finally the discovery of the law of *Varnashrama* is a magnificent result of the ceaseless search for truth. I must not burden this article with definitions of the essentials sketched here, except to say that the present ideas of cow-worship and *Varnashrama* are a caricature of what in my opinion the originals are... In this all too brief a sketch I have mentioned what occurs to me to be the outstanding features of Hinduism that keep me in its fold.

—Gandhi, M.K., 'Why I Am a Hindu', *Young India*, Vol. 9, No. 41, 20 October 1927, p. 352.

5

Sanatani Hindu

I call myself Sanatani Hindu, because I believe in the Vedas, Upanishads, the Puranas and the writings left by the holy reformers. This belief does not require me to accept as authentic everything that passes as Shastras. I reject everything that contradicts the fundamental principles of morality. I am not required to accept the ipse dixit or the interpretations of pundits. Above all I call myself a Sanatani Hindu, so long as the Hindu society in general accepts me as such. In a concrete manner he is a Hindu who believes in God, immortality of the soul, transmigration, the law of Karma and Moksha, and who tries to practise Truth and Ahimsa in daily life, and therefore practises cow-protection in its widest sense and understands and tries to act according to the law of Varnashrama.

—'Correspondence: A Catechism', *Young India*, Vol. 8, No. 41, 14 October 1926, p. 356.

For me Hinduism is all-sufficing. Every variety of belief finds protection under its ample folk.

—Gandhi, M.K., *Speeches And Writings of M.K. Gandhi*, G.A. Natesan and Company, 1922, p. 266.

There is nothing in the world that would keep me from professing Christianity or any other faith, the moment I felt the truth of and the need for it. Where there is fear, there is no religion... If I could call myself, say, a Christian, or a Mussalman, with my own interpretation of the Bible or the Koran, I should not hesitate to call myself either. For then Hindu, Christian and Mussalman would be synonymous terms. I do believe that in the other world there are neither Hindus, nor Christians nor Mussalmans. They all are judged not according to their labels, or professions, but according to their actions, irrespective of their professions. During our earthly existence there will always be these labels. I, therefore, prefer to retain the label of my forefathers so long as it does not cramp my growth and does not debar me from assimilating all that is good anywhere else.

— Gandhi, M.K., 'Crime of Reading Bible', *Young India*, Vol. 8, No. 35, 2 September 1926, p. 308.

'...I know that friends get confused when I say I am a Sanatanist Hindu and they fail to find in me things they associate with a man usually labeled as such. But that is because, in spite of my being a staunch Hindu, I find room in my faith for Christian and Islamic and Zoroastrian teaching, and, therefore, my Hinduism seems to some to be a conglomeration and some have even dubbed me an eclectic. Well, to call a man eclectic is to say that he has no faith, but mine is a broad faith which does not oppose Christians-not even a Plymouth Brother-not even the most fanatical Mussalman. It is a faith based on the broadest possible toleration. I refuse to abuse a man for his fanatical deeds because I try to see them from his point of view. It is that broad faith that sustains me. It is a somewhat embarrassing position, I know-but to others, not to me!'

—Quoted in Desai, Mahadev, 'Ceylon Memories: Things of the Spirit', *Young India*, 22 December 1927, Vol. 9, No. 47, p. 425.

The chief value of Hinduism lies in holding the actual belief that all life (not only human beings, but all sentient beings) is one, i.e., all life coming from the One universal source, call it Allah, God or Parameshwara.

—Gandhi, M.K., *Harijan*, 26 December 1936, p. 365.

My Hinduism is not sectarian. It includes all that I know to be best in Islam, Christianity, Buddhism and Zoroastrianism....Truth is my religion and ahimsa is the only way of its realization. I have rejected once and for all the doctrine of the sword.

—Gandhi, M.K., *Harijan*, 30 April 1938, p. 99.

'Hinduism with its message of ahimsa is to me the most glorious religion in the world—as my wife to me is the most beautiful woman in the world–but others may feel the same about their own religion.'

—Quoted in Desai, Mahadev, 'The Week: Conversion', *Young India*, Vol. 10, No. 1, 19 January 1928, p. 22.

The most distinctive and the largest contribution of Hinduism to India's culture is the doctrine of ahimsa. It has given a definite bias to the history of the country for the last three thousand years and over and it has not ceased to be a living force in the lives of India's millions even today. It is a growing doctrine, its message is still being delivered. Its teaching has so far permeated our people that an armed revolution has almost become an impossibility in India not because, as some would have it, we as a race are physically weak, for it does not require much physical strength so much as a devilish will to press a trigger to shoot a person, but because the tradition of ahimsa has struck deep root among the people.

—Gandhi, M.K., *Harijan,* 24 March 1929, p. 95.

6

My Understanding of Hinduism

Let me explain what I mean by religion. It is not the Hindu religion which I certainly prize above all other religions, but the religion which transcends Hinduism, which changes one's very nature, which binds one indissolubly to the truth within and which ever purifies. It is the permanent element in human nature which counts no cost too great in order to find full expression and which leaves the soul utterly restless until it has found itself, known its Maker and appreciated the true correspondence between the Maker and itself.

—Gandhi, M.K., 'Neither a Saint Nor a Politician', *Young India*, Vol. 2, No. 19, 12 May 1922, p. 2.

There is undoubtedly a sense in which the statement is true when I say that I hold my religion dearer than my country and that, therefore, I am a Hindu first and nationalist after. I do not become on that score a less nationalist than the best of them. I simply thereby imply that the interests of my country are identical with those of my religion. Similarly when I say that I prize my own salvation above everything else, above the salvation of India, it does not mean that my personal salvation requires a sacrifice of India's political or any other salvation. But it implies necessarily that the two go together.

—Gandhi, M.K., 'No End to my Sorrows', *Young India*, Vol. 4, No. 8, 23 February 1922, p. 123.

I am not a literalist. Therefore I try to understand the *spirit* of the various scriptures of the world. I apply the test of Truth and Ahimsa laid down by these very scriptures for interpretation. I reject what is inconsistent with that test, and I appropriate all that is consistent with it. The story of a Sudra having been punished by Ramachandra for daring to learn the Vedas I reject as an interpolation. And in any event, I worship Rama, the perfect being of my conception, not a historical person facts about whose life may vary with the progress of new historical discoveries and researches. Tulsidas had nothing to do with the Rama of history. Judged by historical test, his Ramayana would be fit for the scrap heap. As a spiritual experience, his book is almost unrivalled at least for me. And then, too, I do not swear by every word that is to be found in so many editions published as the Ramayana of Tulsidas. It is the spirit running through the book that holds me spellbound. I cannot myself subscribe to the prohibition against Sudras learning the Vedas. Indeed, in my opinion, at the present moment, we are all predominantly Sudras, so long as we are serfs. Knowledge cannot be the prerogative of any class or section. But I can conceive the impossibility of people assimilating higher or subtler truths unless they have undergone preliminary training, even as those who have not made preliminary preparations are quite unfit to breathe the rarefied atmosphere in high altitudes, or those who have no preliminary training in simple mathematics are unfit to understand or assimilate higher Geometry or Algebra. Lastly, I believe in certain healthy conventions. There is a convention surrounding the recitation of the *Gayatri*. The convention is that it should be recited only at stated times and after ablutions performed in the prescribed manner. As I believe in those conventions, and as I am not able always to conform to them, for years past I have followed the later Saints, and therefore have satisfied myself with the *Dwadasha Mantra* of the Bhagawat or the still simpler formula of Tulsidas and a few selections from the Gita and other works, and a few bhajanas in *Prakrit*. These are my daily spiritual food—my *Gayatri*. They give me all the peace and solace I need from day to day.

—Gandhi, M.K., 'Notes: Sanatana Hindu', *Young India*, Vol. 7, No. 35, 27 August 1925, p. 293.

7

Fasting in Satyagraha

I do not know any contemporary of mine who has reduced fasting and prayer to an exact science and who reaped a harvest so abundant as I have. I wish that I could infect the nation with my experience and make it resort to fasting and prayer with intelligence, honesty and intensity. We would thus, incredible as it may appear, do millions of things pertaining to the nation without elaborate organization and checks upon checks, but I know that fasting and prayer, to be as effective as I have found them to be in my own experience, have to be not mechanical things but definite spiritual acts. Fasting then is crucifixion of the flesh with a corresponding freedom of the spirit and prayer is a definite conscious longing of the soul to the utterly pure—the purity thus attained being dedicated to the realization of a particular object which is in itself pure.

—*The Collected Works of Mahatma Gandhi (digital)*,
Vol. XVII, Publications Division Government of India,
New Delhi, 2005.

Fasting in Satyagraha has well-defined limits. You cannot fast against a tyrant, for it will be as a piece of violence done to him. You invite penalty from him for disobedience of his orders, but you cannot inflict on yourself penalties when he refuses to punish and renders it impossible for you to disobey his orders so as to compel infliction of penalty. Fasting can only be restored to against a lover, not to extort rights but to reform him, as when a son fasts for a parent who drinks. My fast at Bombay, and then at Bardoli, was of that character. I fasted to reform those who loved me. But I will not fast to reform, say, General Dyer who not only does not love me, but who regards himself as my enemy.

—*The Collected Works of Mahatma Gandhi (digital)*, Vol. XVIII, Publications Division Government of India, New Delhi, 2005.

Fasting should be inspired by perfect truth and perfect non-violence. The call for it should come from within and it should not be imitative. It should never be undertaken for a selfish purpose, but for the benefit of others only. A fast is out of the question in a case where there is hatred for anybody. But what is the inner voice? Is every one capable of hearing it? These are big questions. The inner voice is there in every one of us, but one whose ears are not open for it cannot hear it, just as a deaf person is unable to hear the sweetest of songs. Self-restraint is essential in order to make our ears fit to hear the voice of God.

—Gandhi, M.K., *Selected Letters: Second Series*, Valji Govindji Desai (trans.), Navajivan Publishing House, 1962, pp. 46–47.

8

Between Violence and Cowardice

I do believe that, where there is only a choice between cowardice and violence, I would advise violence. Thus when my eldest son asked me what he should have done, had he been present when I was almost fatally assaulted in 1908, whether he should have run away and seen me killed or whether he should have used his physical force which he could and wanted to use, and defended me, I told him that it was his duty to defend me even by using violence.

But I believe that non-violence is infinitely superior to violence, forgiveness is more manly than punishment. Forgiveness adorns a soldier. But abstinence is forgiveness only when there is the power to punish; it is meaningless when it pretends to proceed from a helpless creature. A mouse hardly forgives a cat when it allows itself to be torn to pieces by her. I therefore appreciate the sentiment of those who cry out for the condign punishment of General Dyer and his ilk. They would tear him to pieces, if they could. But I do not believe India to be helpless. I do not believe myself to be a helpless creature. Only I want to use India's and my strength for a better purpose.

Let me not be misunderstood. Strength does not come from physical capacity. It comes from an indomitable will. An average Zulu is any way more than a match for an average Englishman in bodily capacity. But he flees from an English boy, because he fears the boy's revolver or those who will use it for him. He fears death and is nerveless in spite of his burly figure. We in India may in a moment realize that one hundred thousand Englishmen need not frighten three hundred million human beings. A definite forgiveness would, therefore, mean a definite recognition of our strength. With enlightened forgiveness must come a mighty wave of strength in us, which would make it impossible for a Dyer and a Frank Johnson to heap affront on India's devoted head. It matters little to me that for the moment I do not drive my point home. We feel too down-trodden not to be angry and revengeful. But I must not refrain from saying that India can gain more by waiving the right of punishment. We have better work to do, a better mission to deliver to the world.

I am not a visionary. I claim to be a practical idealist. The religion of non-violence is not meant merely for the Rishis and saints. It is meant for the common people as well. Non-violence is the law of our species as violence is the law of the brute. The spirit lies dormant in the brute, and he knows no law but that of physical might. The dignity of man requires obedience to a higher law—to the strength of the spirit.

I have therefore ventured to place before India the ancient law of self-sacrifice. For Satyagraha and its offshoots, non-co-operation and civil resistance, are nothing but new names for the law of suffering. The Rishis, who discovered the law of non-violence in the midst of violence, were greater geniuses than Newton. They were themselves greater warriors than Wellington. Having themselves known the use of arms, they realized their uselessness, and taught a weary world that its salvation lay not through violence but through non-violence.

Non-violence in its dynamic condition means conscious suffering. It does not mean meek submission to the will of the evil-doer, but it means putting of one's whole soul against the will of the tyrant. Working under this law of our being, it is possible for a single individual to defy the whole might of an unjust empire to save his honour, his religion, his soul, and lay the foundation for that empire's fall or its regeneration.

And so I am not pleading for India to practise nonviolence because she is weak. I want her to practise nonviolence being conscious of her strength and power. No training in arms is required for realization of her strength. We seem to need it, because we seem to think that we are but a lump of flesh. I want India to recognize that she has a soul that cannot perish, and that can rise triumphant above every physical weakness and defy the physical combination of a whole world. What is the meaning of Rama, a mere human being, with his host of monkeys, pitting himself against the insolent strength of ten-headed Ravana surrounded in supposed safety by the raging waters on all sides of Lanka? Does it not mean the conquest of physical might by spiritual strength? However, being a practical man, I do not wait till India recognizes the practicability of the spiritual life in the political world. India considers herself to be powerless and paralyzed before the machine guns, the tanks and the aeroplanes of the English, and takes up non-co-operation out of her weakness. It must still serve the same purpose, namely, bring her delivery from the crushing weight of British injustice, if a sufficient number of people practise it.

If India takes up the doctrine of the sword, she may gain momentary victory. Then India will cease to be the pride of my heart. I am wedded to India because I owe my all to her. I believe absolutely that she has a mission for the world. She is not to copy Europe blindly. India's acceptance of the doctrine of the sword will be the hour of my trial. I hope I shall not be found wanting. My religion has no geographical limits. If I have a living faith in it, it will transcend my love for India herself. My life is dedicated to the service of India through the religion of non-violence which I believe to be the root of Hinduism.

—Gandhi, M.K., *Young India*, 11 August 1920.

Let us confine ourselves to Ahimsa. We have all along regarded the spinning wheel, village crafts, etc. as the pillars of Ahimsa, and so indeed they are. They must stand. But we have now to go a step further. A votary of Ahimsa will of course base upon non-violence, if he has not already done so, all his relations with his parents, his children, his wife, his servants, his dependants, etc. But the real test will come at the time of political or communal disturbances or under the menace of thieves and dacoits. Mere resolve to lay down one's life under the circumstances is not enough. There must be the necessary qualification for making the sacrifice. If I am a Hindu, I must fraternize with the Musalmans and the rest. In my dealing with them I may not make any distinction between my coreligionists and those who might belong to a different faith. I would seek opportunities to serve them without any feeling of fear or unnaturalness. The word 'fear' can have no place in the dictionary of Ahimsa. Having thus qualified himself by his selfless service, a votary of pure Ahimsa will be in a position to make a fit offering of himself in a communal conflagration. Similarly, to meet the menace of thieves and dacoits, he will need to go among, and cultivate friendly relations with the communities from which thieves and dacoits generally come.

A brilliant example of this kind of work is provided by Ravishankar Maharaj. His work among the criminal tribes in Gujarat has evoked praise even of the Baroda State authorities. There is an almost unlimited field for this kind of work, and it does not call for any other talent in one besides pure love. Ravishankar Maharaj is an utter stranger to English. Even his knowledge of Gujarati is barely sufficient for everyday use. But God has blessed him with unlimited neighbourly love. His simplicity easily wins all hearts, and is the envy of everybody. Let his example provide a cue and inspiration to all those who may be similarly engaged in other fields of Satyagraha.

—Gandhi, M.K., *Harijan*, 21 July 1940.

9

Cow Worship in Hinduism

Cow protection is the dearest possession of the Hindu heart... No one who does not believe in cow protection can possibly be a Hindu. It is a noble belief... Cow worship means to me worship of innocence. For me, the cow is the personification of innocence. Cow protection means the protection of the weak and the helpless. As professor Vaswani truly remarks, cow protection means brotherhood between man and beast. It is a noble sentiment that must grow by patient toil and *tapasya*.

—Gandhi, M.K., 'Save the Cow', *Young India*, Vol. 3, No. 22, 8 June 1921, p. 182.

Cow protection to me is one of the most wonderful phenomena in human evolution. It takes the human being beyond his species. The cow to me means the entire subhuman world. Man through the cow is enjoined to realize his identity with all that lives. Why the cow was selected for apotheosis is obvious to me. The cow was in India the best companion. She was the giver of plenty. Not only did she give milk but she also made agriculture possible. The cow is a poem of pity. One reads pity in the gentle animal. She is the mother to millions of Indian mankind. Protection of the cow means protection of the whole dumb creation of God. The ancient seer, whoever he was, began with the cow. The appeal of the lower order of creation is all the more forcible because it is speechless. Cow protection is the gift of Hinduism to the world. And Hinduism will live so long as there are Hindus to protect the cow.

> —Gandhi, M.K., 'Hinduism', *Young India*, Vol. 3, No. 40, 6 October 1921, pp. 317–19.

[O]ur *Rishis* made the startling discovery, (and every day I feel more and more convinced of its truth) that sacred texts and inspired writings yield their truth only in proportion as one has advanced in the practice of *Ahimsa* and truth. The greater the realization of truth and *Ahimsa* the greater the illumination. These same *Rishis* declared that cow protection was the supreme duty of a Hindu and that its performance brought one *Moksha*, i.e. salvation. Now I am not ready to believe that by merely protecting the animal cow, one can attain *Moksha*. For *Moksha* one must completely get rid of one's lower feelings like attachment, hatred, anger, jealousy, etc. It follows, therefore, that the meaning of cow protection in terms of *Moksha* must be much wider and far more comprehensive than is commonly supposed. The cow protection which can bring one *Moksha* must, from its very nature, include the protection of everything that feels. Therefore, in my opinion, every little breach of the *Ahimsa* principle, like causing hurt by harsh speech to any one, man, woman or child, to cause pain to the weakest and the most insignificant creature on earth would be a breach of the principle of cow protection, would be tantamount to the sin of beef-eating, differing from it in degree, if at all, rather than in kind.

—Gandhi, M.K., 'Cow Protection', *Young India*, Vol. 7, No. 5, 29 January 1925, pp. 337–39.

A Hindu who protects the cow should protect every animal. But taking all things into consideration, we may not cavil at his protecting the cow because he fails to protect the other animals. The only question therefore to consider is whether he is right in protecting the cow. And he cannot be wrong in so doing if non-killing of animals generally may be regarded as a duty for one who believes in *ahimsa*. And every Hindu, and for that matter every man of religion, does so. The duty of not killing animals generally and therefore protecting them must be accepted as an indisputable fact. It is then so much to the credit of Hinduism that it has taken up cow protection as a duty. And he is a poor specimen of Hinduism who stops merely at cow protection when he can extend the arm of protection to other animals. The cow merely stands as a symbol, and protection of the cow is the least he is expected to undertake…

The motive that actuates cow protection is not 'purely selfish', though selfish consideration undoubtedly enters into it. If it was purely selfish, the cow would be killed as in other countries after it had ceased to give full use. The Hindus will not kill the cow even though she may be a heavy burden. The numberless Goshalas that have been established by charitably-minded people for tending [to] disabled and useless cows is in a way an eloquent testimony of the effort that is being made in the direction. Though they are today very poor institutions for the object to be achieved the fact does not detract from the value of the motive behind the act.

The philosophy of cow protection, therefore, is in my opinion sublime. It immediately puts the animal creation on the same level with man so far as the right to live is concerned.

—Gandhi, M.K., 'Cow Protection', *Young India*, Vol. 8, No. 45, 11 November 1926, pp. 337–39.

10

Cow Protection

[T]he cow is the purest type of sub-human life. She pleads before us on behalf of the whole of the sub-human species for justice to it at the hands of man, the first among all that lives. She seems to speak to us through her eyes: 'you are not appointed over us to kill us and eat our flesh or otherwise ill-treat us, but to be our friend and guardian'.

—Gandhi, M.K., *Young India*, 26 June 1924, p. 214.

I worship it and I shall defend its worship against the whole world.

—Gandhi, M.K., *Young India*, 1 January 1925, p. 8.

Mother cow is in many ways better than the mother who gave us birth. Our mother gives us milk for a couple of years and then expects us to serve her when we grow up. Mother cow expects from us nothing but grass and grain. Our mother often falls ill and expects service from us. Mother cow rarely falls ill. Here is an unbroken record of service which does not end with her death. Our mother, when she dies, means expenses of burial or cremation. Mother cow is as useful dead as when she is alive. We can make use of every part of her body-her flesh, her bones, her intestines, her horns and her skin. Well, I say this not to disparage the mother who gives us birth, but in order to show you the substantial reasons for my worshipping the cow.

—Gandhi, M.K., *Harijan*, 15 September 1940, p. 281.

The central fact of Hinduism is cow protection. Cow protection to me is one of the most wonderful phenomena in human evolution. It takes the human being beyond this species. The cow to me means the entire sub-human world. Man through the cow is enjoined to realize his identity with all that lives. Why the cow was selected for apotheosis is obvious to me. The cow was in India the best companion. She was the giver of plenty. Not only did she give milk, but she also made agriculture possible...

Hindus will be judged not by their *tilaks*, not by the correct chanting of *mantras*, not by their pilgrimages, not by their most punctilious observances of caste rules, but their ability to protect the cow.

—Gandhi, M.K., *Young India*, 6 October 1921, p. 36.

I would not kill a human being for protection a cow, as I will not kill a cow for saving a human life, be it ever so precious.

—Gandhi, M.K., *Young India*, 18 May 1921, p. 156.

My religion teaches me that I should by personal conduct instill into the minds of those who might hold different views, the conviction that cow-killing is a sin and that, therefore, it ought to be abandoned.

—Gandhi, M.K., *Young India*, 29 January 1925, p. 38.

Cow slaughter can never be stopped by law. Knowledge,

education, and the spirit of kindliness towards her alone can put and end to it. It will not be possible to save those animals that are a burden on the land or, perhaps, even man if he is a burden.

—Gandhi, M.K., *Harijan*, 15 September 1946, p. 310.

My ambition is no less than to see the principle of cow protection established throughout the world. But that requires that I should set my own house thoroughly in order first.

—Gandhi, M.K., *Young India*, 29 January 1925, p. 38.

Cow protection to me is not mere protection of the cow. It means protection of that lives and is helpless and weak in the world.

—Gandhi, M.K., *Young India*, 7 May 1925, p. 160.

But let me reiterate [...] that legislative prohibition is the smallest part of any programme of cow protection... People seem to think that, when a law is passed against any evil, it will die without any further effort. There never was a grosser self-deception. Legislation is intended and is effective against an ignorant or a small, evil-minded minority; but no legislation which is opposed by an intelligent and organized public opinion, or under cover of religion by a fanatical minority, can ever succeed. The more I study the question of cow protection, the stronger the conviction grows upon me that protection of the cow and her progeny can be attained only if there is continuous and sustained constructive effort along the lines suggested by me.

—Gandhi, M.K., *Young India*, 7 July 1927, p. 219.

Preservation of cattle is a vital part of *goseva*. It is a vital question for India... There is urgent need for deep study and the spirit of sacrifice. To amass money and dole out charity does not connote real business capacity. To know how to preserve cattle, to impart this knowledge to the millions, to live up to the ideal oneself, and to spend money on this endeavor is real business.

—Gandhi, M.K., *Harijan*, 17 February 1946, p. 11.

Then, how can the cow be save without having to kill her off when she ceases to give the economic quantity of milk or when one becomes otherwise an uneconomic burden? The answer to the question can be summed up as follows:

By the Hindus performing their duty towards the cow and her progeny. If they did so, our cattle would be the pride of India and the world. The contrary is the case today.

By learning the science of cattle-breeding. Today there is perfect anarchy in this work.

By replacing the present cruel method of castration by the humane method practiced in the West.

By thorough reform of the *pinjrapoles* [institutions for aged cows] of India which are today, as a rule, managed ignorantly and without any plan by men who do not know their work.

When these primary things are done, it will be found that the Muslims will, of their own accord, recognize the necessity, if only for the sake of their Hindus brethren, of not slaughtering cattle for beef or otherwise.

The reader will observe that behind the foregoing requirements lies one thing and that is *ahimsa*, otherwise known as universal compassion. If that supreme thing is realized, everything else becomes easy. Where there is *ahimsa*, there is *infinite* patience, inner calm, discrimination, self-sacrifice and true knowledge.

—Gandhi, M.K., *Harijan*, 31 August 1947, p. 300.

11

Brahmacharya: The Virtue of Chastity

If it is contended that birth control is necessary for the nation because of over-population, I dispute the proposition. It has never been proved. In my opinion by a proper land system, better agriculture and a supplementary industry, this country is capable of supporting twice as many people as there are in it today.

—Gandhi, M.K., 'Some Arguments Considered', *Young India*, Vol. 7, No. 14, 2 April 1925, pp. 117–18.

What, then, is *Brahmacharya*? It means that men and women should refrain from carnal knowledge of each other. That is to say, they should not touch each other with a carnal thought, they should not think of it even in their dreams. Their mutual glances should be free from all suggestion of carnality. The hidden strength that God has given us should be conserved by rigid self-discipline, and transmitted into energy and power—not merely of body, but also of mind and soul.

But what is the spectacle that we actually see around us? Men and women, old and young, without exception, are caught in the meshes of sensuality. Blinded for the most part by lust, they lose all sense of right and wrong. I have myself seen even boys and girls behaving as if they were mad under its fatal influence. I too have behaved likewise under similar influences, and it could not well be otherwise. For the sake of a momentary pleasure, we sacrifice in an instant all the stock of vital energy that we have laboriously accumulated. The infatuation over, we find ourselves in a miserable condition. The next morning we feel hopelessly weak and tired, and the mind refuses to do its work. Then in order to remedy the mischief, we consume large quantities of milk, *bhasmas, yakutis* and what not. We take all sorts of 'nervine tonics' and place ourselves at the doctor's mercy for repairing the waste, and for recovering the capacity for enjoyment. So the days pass and years, until at length old age comes upon us, and find us utterly emasculated in body and in mind.

But the law of Nature is just the reverse of this. The older we grow the keener should our intellect be; the longer we live the greater should be our capacity to communicate the benefit of our accumulated experience to our fellow men. And such is indeed the case with those who have been true *Brahmacharis*. They know no fear of death, and they do not forget God even in the hour of death; nor do they indulge in vain desires. They die with a smile on their lips, and boldly face the day of judgment. They are true men and women; and of them alone can it be said that they have conserved their health.

We hardly realize the fact that incontinence is the root cause of most vanity, anger, fear and jealousy in the world. If our mind is not under our control, if we behave once or oftener every day more foolishly than even little children, what sins may we not commit consciously or unconsciously? How can we pause to think of the consequences of our actions, however vile or sinful they may be?

But you may ask, 'Who has ever seen a true *Brahmachari* in this sense? If all men should turn Brahmacharis, would not humanity be extinct and the whole world go to rack and ruin? We will leave aside the religious aspect of this question and discuss it simply from the secular point of view. To my mind, these questions only betray our timidity and worse. We have not the strength of will to observe *Brahmacharya*, and therefore set about finding pretexts for evading our duty. The race of true *Brahmacharis* is by no means extinct; but if they were commonly to be met with, of what value would *Brahmacharya* be? Thousands of hardy labourers have to go and dig deep into the bowels of the earth in search for diamonds, and at length they get perhaps merely a handful of them out of heaps and heaps of rock. How much greater, then, should be the labour involved in the discovery of the infinitely more precious diamond of a *Brahmachari*? If the observance of *Brahmacharya* should mean the end of the world, that is none of our business. Are we God that we should be so anxious about its future? He who created it will surely see to its preservation. We need not trouble to inquire whether other people practice *Brahmacharya* or not. When we enter a trade or profession, do we ever pause to consider what the fate of the world would be if all men were to do likewise? The true *Brahmachari* will, in the long run, discover for himself answer to such questions.

But how can men engrossed in the cares of the material world put these ideas into practice? What about those who are married? What shall they do who have children? And what shall be done by those people who cannot control themselves? We have already seen what is the highest state for us to attain. We should keep this ideal constantly before us, and try to approach it to the utmost of our capacity. When little children are taught to write the letters of the alphabet, we show them the perfect shapes of the letters, and they try to reproduce them as best they can. In the same way, if we steadily work up to the ideal of *Brahmacharya* we may ultimately succeed in realizing it. What if we have married already? The law of Nature is that *Brahmacharya* may be broken only when the husband and wife feel a desire for progeny. Those, who, remembering this law, violate *Brahmacharya* once in four or five years, will not become slaves to lust, nor lose much of their stock of vital energy. But, alas! How rare are those men and women who yield to the sexual craving merely for the sake of offspring! The vast majority turn to sexual enjoyment merely to satisfy their carnal passion, with the result that children are born to them quite against their will. In the madness of sexual passion, they give no thought to the consequences of their acts. In this respect, men are even more to blame than women. The man is blinded so much by his lust that he never cares to remember that his wife is weak and unable to bear or rear up a child...

Our diet, our ways of life, our common talk, and our environments are all equally calculated to rouse animal passions; and sensuality is like a poison eating into our vitals. Some people may doubt the possibility of our being able to free ourselves from this bondage...

From all that has been said it follows that those who are still unmarried should try to remain so; but if they cannot help marrying, they should defer it as long as possible.

Young men, for instance, should take a vow to remain unmarried till the age of twenty-five or thirty. We cannot consider here all the advantages other than physical which they will reap and which are as it were added unto the rest.

—Gandhi, M.K., *Self-restraint v. Self-indulgence*, Navajivan Publishing House, 1928.

12

Hindu Code of Conduct

1. If we are not in the habit of waking up before dawn, it should be formed.
2. There are many people who start smoking the moment they wake up, others, little better, make the whole house aware of their having woken up by talking profanities. Instead of this, one should recite the name of God before leaving the bed and thank Him for the night having passed safely.
3. After leaving the bed we should immediately awaken our children and then, sitting in a place which is not crowded, we should clean our teeth with babul or some other twig. We should use either salt or powdered charcoal which we should keep ready at home to clean our teeth and with the halves of the twig we should scrape the tongue and rinse the mouth well. We should splash water over our eyes and remove mucus if there is any. Having done that we must wash our face, nose, ears, etc., carefully and wipe with a clean cloth.
4. If one has to evacuate one's bowels and that particular village has no latrine, or if there is one, but one does not like to use it, this function should be performed in a remote place which is not crowded. The excreta should be properly covered with mud and the organs

concerned should be properly cleansed with water. As both the excretory organs throw out waste, these should be properly cleansed and the waste material eliminated. Thereafter the hands should be washed with water and mud, and the water-pot should also be cleaned well.

5. While performing this daily routine one should either hum Ramdhun or any devotional song. If one does not know any of these, one should merely keep repeating the name of Rama.

6. It would be daylight by the time one returns home. Other members of the family would also have performed their natural functions as mentioned above. All should then get together and sing bhajans or do kirtan for five minutes to half an hour. So long as one does not know any such thing, one can at least repeat the name of Rama.

7. Thereafter, everyone should set out for work after having breakfast. Children who do not work should go to school.

8. Before taking the midday meal, everyone should bathe with clean water and scrub the whole body. Dhoti, sari and any other garments should be washed. The poor who do not have the facility of changing daily should wear a loin-cloth while bathing. The body should be rubbed and wiped after a bath.

9. Thereafter, when night falls after performing one's daily tasks, God's name should be uttered after the evening meal and before going to bed and He should be thanked that the day passed without any mishap.

10. The hands should be washed properly after every meal and after undertaking any task which soils the hands.

After a meal, one should gargle and rinse one's mouth.

11. We should acknowledge that God knows our every thought and sees everything we do. Hence, no one can deceive Him. How then can we deceive our brothers and sisters who are His creatures? It may well be that these people are unaware of our deception. If they come to know of the latter, how can we cheat them at all?

12. Hence, we should dedicatedly serve those under whom we work and not deceive them.

13. And, if we can not deceive anyone, how can we commit any theft? Even defrauding while weighing goods amounts to theft.

14. We would not like anyone to abuse us, beat us or misbehave with our mothers or sisters. Therefore, we should not abuse anyone, not even our wives and children.

15. Nor should we beat anyone including wives and children. These people have to be separately mentioned because many men regard their wives and children as their property. But it is a grave error. In our religion, wives have been regarded equal to the husband. Hence, she is known as the other half, co-partner in religion and a goddess. Children are not our property. Parents are the protectors of children. Hence, even with them, we should be gentle, tolerant and patient.

16. Just as we should have goodwill towards our wives and children, similarly elders and parents should be treated with respect.

17. And, as shown in 14 above, it is implied that a man should treat another man's wife as his sister or mother

and, similarly, a woman should regard another man as her father or brother.
18. Just as all men are creatures of God, so are animals; hence, they are also a part of our family. We should therefore be good towards them as well. We should not misuse even mud or stones. Our religion teaches us such prayer: "Oh! Mother Earth, we walk upon you every day. We depend upon your support. Forgive us for touching you with our feet." Having said this, we put a pinch of dust upon our heads.
19. And hence we should be kind towards our animals; we should feed them properly; we should not overload them with burdens, we should keep them in clean spaces; and refrain from hurting them.
20. Similarly, we should pluck leaves and cut trees only as much as we absolutely have to. We should use discretion while doing so and should not destroy wantonly.
21. So far as possible, we should avoid eating meat. Beef should be totally shunned. Cow-protection is situated at a very fundamental spot in our religion.
22. In accordance with clause 19, all living creatures are our brothers and sisters. Our rishis and munis taught us to regard cow as our mother and that we should develop friendly relations towards all living beings including non-human creatures. It is in the fitness of things to regard cow as our mother as she, like a mother, gives us milk. One who gets milk does not require fish or meat. Moreover, cow provides us with bullocks and even after dying gives us leather, manure, fat for carts, etc., and other things. Hence, we should never kill a cow.

23. And if we can't kill a cow, how can we eat the flesh after her death? No sensible people in the world eat carrion.
24. By becoming an addict, a man renders himself metaphorically insane; at times, he completely loses his senses. Hence liquor, toddy, bhang, ganja, opium and tobacco should be renounced.
25. Gambling involves befooling and the money obtained through it is ill-gotten. Hence, we should not gamble.
26. Others are as fond of their religion as we are of ours. Hence, all religions should equally be respected. We should bear no ill will or have disputes with Muslims, Christians or followers of other faiths.
27. If religion teaches us that we are all children of God, there can be no high or low among them and there should not be even the slightest trace of untouchability.
28. Finally, our religion also tells us that anyone who does not earn his living with sweat and blood, eats stolen food. Hence, everyone should earn bread by engaging in such manual tasks as farming, or making cloth, etc., and it is for this very reason that each person should produce food grains, khadi and such other articles of food and clothing in their own village.

These are the things which I have often said on several occasions have been put down in writing here. Other clauses may be added to these as and when the occasion arises bearing in mind the universal elements like truth and non-violence, which are involved in them.

—Gandhi, M.K., *Harijanbandhu*, 27 December 1936.

13

Contemporary Hinduism

Hinduism is a living organism liable to growth and decay, and subject to the laws of Nature. One and indivisible at the root, it has grown into a vast tree with innumerable branches. The changes in the seasons affect it. It has its autumn and summer, its winter and spring. The rains nourish and fructify it too. It is and is not based on scriptures. It does not derive its authority from one book. The Gita is universally accepted, but even then it only shows the way. It has hardly any effect on custom. Hinduism is like the Ganges, pure and unsullied at its source, but taking in its course the impurities in the way. Even like the Ganga it is beneficent in its total effect. It takes a provincial form in every province, but the inner substance is retained everywhere. Custom is not religion. Custom may change, but religion will remain unaltered.

—Gandhi, M.K., 'Hinduism of Today', *Young India*, Vol. 8, No. 14, 8 April 1926, p. 131.

Purity of Hinduism depends on the self-restraint of its votaries. Whenever their religion has been in danger, the Hindus have undergone rigorous penance, searched the causes of the danger and devised means for combating them. The shastras are ever growing. The Vedas, the

Upanishads, the Smritis, the Puranas, and the Itihasas did not arise at one and the same time. Each grew out of the necessities of particular periods, and therefore they seem to conflict with one another. These books do not enunciate anew the eternal truths but show how these were practised at the time to which the books belong. A practice which was good enough in a particular period would, if blindly repeated in another, land people into the 'slough of despond'. Because the practice of animal-sacrifice obtained at one time, shall we revive it today? Because at one time we used to eat beef, shall we also do so now? Because at one time, we used to chop off the hands and feet of thieves, shall we revive that barbarity today? Shall we revive polyandry? Shall we revive child-marriage? Because we discarded a section of humanity one day, shall we brand their descendants today as outcasts?

Hinduism abhors stagnation. Knowledge is limitless and so also the application of truth. Everyday we add to our knowledge of the power of Atman, and we shall keep on doing so. New experience will teach us new duties, but truth shall ever be the same. Who has ever known it in its entirety? The Vedas represent the truth, they are infinite. But who has known them in their entirety? What goes today by the name of the Vedas are not even a millionth part of the real Veda—the Book of Knowledge. And who knows the entire meaning of even the few books that we have? Rather than wade through these infinite complications, our sages taught us to learn one thing: 'As with the Self, so with the Universe'. It is not possible to scan the universe, as it is to scan the self. Know the self and you know the universe. But even knowledge of the self within presupposes ceaseless striving—not only ceaseless but pure, and pure striving presupposes a pure heart, which in its turn depends on the practice of *yamas*[1] and *niyamas*—the cardinal and casual virtues.

This practice is not possible without God's grace which presupposes Faith and Devotion. This is why Tulsidas sang of the glory of *Ramanama*, that is why the author of the Bhagawata taught the *Dwadashamantra* (*Om Namo Bhagawate Vasudevaya*). To my mind he is a Sanatani Hindu who can repeat this mantra from the heart. All else is a bottomless pit, as the sage Akho[2] has said...

[...] Hinduism does not consist in eating and non-eating. Its kernel consists in right conduct, in correct observance of truth and non-violence. Many a man eating meat, but observing the cardinal virtues of compassion and truth, and living in the fear of God, is a better Hindu than a hypocrite who abstains from meat. And he whose eyes are opened to the truth of the violence in beef-eating or meat-eating and who has therefore rejected them, who loves 'both man and bird and beast' is worthy of our adoration. He has seen and known God; he is His best devotee. He is the teacher of mankind.

Hinduism and all other religions are being weighed in the balance. Eternal truth is one. God also is one. Let

---

[1] Yamas, the cardinal virtues, according to Yogashastra, are Ahimsa (non-violence), Satya (truth), Asteya (non-stealing), Brahmacharya (celibacy), Aparigraha (non-possession). The Niyamas or the casual virtues are, according to the same authority, Shaucha (bodily purity), Santosha (contentment), Tapa (forbearance), Swadhyaya (study of scriptures), Ishivarapranidhana (resignation to the will of God).
[2] A poet-seer of Gujarat.

every one of us steer clear of conflicting creeds and customs and follow the straight path of truth. Only then shall we be true Hindus. Many styling themselves *sanatanis* stalk the earth. Who knows how few of them will be chosen by God? God's grace shall descend on those who do His will and wait upon Him, not on those who simply mutter 'Ram Ram'.

—Gandhi, M.K., 'Hinduism of Today', *Young India*, Vol. 8, No. 14, 8 April 1926, p. 131.

In the name of religion we Hindus have made a fetish of outward observances and have degraded religion by making it simply a question of eating and drinking. Brahmanism owes its unrivalled position to its self-abnegation, its inward purity, its severe austerity—all these illumined by knowledge. Hindus are doomed if they attach undue importance to the spiritual effects of foods and human contacts. Placed as we are in the midst of trials and temptations from within, and touched and polluted as we are by all the most untouchable and the vilest thought currents, let us not, in our arrogance, exaggerate the influence of contact with people whom we often ignorantly and more often arrogantly consider to be our inferiors. Before the Throne of the Almighty we shall be judged, not by what we have eaten nor by whom we have been touched by but by whom we have served and how. Inasmuch as we serve a single human being in distress, we shall find favour in the sight of God. Bad and stimulating or dirty foods we must avoid as we must avoid bad contact. But let us not give these observances a place out of all proportion to their importance. We dare not use abstinence from certain foods as a cover for fraud, hypocrisy, and worse vices. We dare not refuse to serve a fallen or a dirty brother lest his contact should injure our spiritual growth.

—Gandhi, M.K., 'The Congress and After', *Young India*, Vol. 4, No. 1, 5 January 1922, p. 3.

14

Misinterpretation of Hinduism

What we see to-day is not pure Hinduism, but often a parody of it. Otherwise it would require no pleading from me in its behalf, but would speak for itself, even as if I was absolutely pure I would not need to speak to you. God does not speak with His tongue, and man in the measure that he comes near God becomes like God. Hinduism teaches me that my body is a limitation of the power of the soul within.

Just as in the West they have made wonderful discoveries in things material, similarly Hinduism has made still more marvellous discoveries in things of religion, of the spirit, of the soul. But we have no eye for these great and fine discoveries. We are dazzled by the material progress that Western science has made. I am not enamoured of that progress. In fact, it almost seems as though God in His wisdom had prevented India from progressing along those lines, so that it might fulfil its special mission of resisting the onrush of materialism. After all, there is something in Hinduism that has kept it alive up till now. It has witnessed the fall of Babylonian, Syrian, Persian and Egyptian civilizations. Cast a look round you. Where is Rome and Greece? Can you find today anywhere the Italy of Gibbon, or rather the ancient Rome, for Rome was Italy? Go to

Greece. Where is the world-famous Attic civilization? Then come to India, let one go through the most ancient records and then look round you and you would be constrained to say, 'Yes, I see here ancient India still living.' True, there are dungheaps, too, here and there, but there are rich treasures buried under them. And the reason why it has survived is that the end which Hinduism set before it was not development along material but spiritual lines.

Among its many contributions the idea of man's identity with the dumb creation is a unique one. To me cow-worship is a great idea which is capable of expansion. The freedom of Hinduism from the modern proselytization is also to me a precious thing. It needs no preaching. It says, 'Live the life.' It is my business, it is your business to live the life, and then we will leave its influence on ages. Then take its contribution in men: Ramanuja, Chaitanya, Ramakrishna, not to speak of the more modern names, have left their impress on Hinduism. Hinduism is by no means a spent force or a dead religion.

Then there is the contribution of the four *ashramas*, again a unique contribution. There is nothing like it in the whole world. The Catholics have the order of celibates corresponding to *brahmacharis*, but not as an institution, whereas in India every boy had to go through the first *ashrama*. What a grand conception it was! Today our eyes are dirty, thoughts dirtier and bodies dirtiest of all, because we are denying Hinduism.

There is yet another thing I have not mentioned. Max Muller said forty years ago that it was dawning on Europe that transmigration is not a theory, but a fact. Well, it is entirely the contribution of Hinduism.

Today *varnashramadharma* and Hinduism are misrepresented and denied by its votaries. The remedy is not destruction, but correction. Let us reproduce in ourselves the true Hindu spirit, and then ask whether it satisfies the soul or not.

—Gandhi, M.K., 'Brahman Non Brahman Question', *Young India*, Vol. 9, No. 26, 24 November 1927, p. 396.

15

Beyond Religious Boundaries

There is in Hinduism room enough for Jesus, as there is for Mohammed, Zoroaster and Moses. For me the different religions are beautiful flowers from the same garden, or they are branches of the same majestic tree. Therefore they are equally true, though being received and interpreted through human instruments equally imperfect.

It is impossible for me to reconcile myself to the idea of conversion after the style that goes on in India and elsewhere today. It is an error which is perhaps the greatest impediment to the world's progress; towards peace. 'Warring creeds' is a blasphemous expression. And it fitly describes the state of things in India, the mother, as I believe her to be, of Religion or religions. If she is truly the mother, the motherhood is on trial. Why should a Christian want to convert a Hindu to Christianity and vice versa? Why should he not be satisfied if the Hindu is a good or godly man?

If the morals of a man are a matter of no concern, the form of worship in a particular manner in a church, a mosque or a temple is an empty formula; it may even be a hindrance to individual or social growth, and insistences on a particular form or repetition of a credo may be a potent cause of violent quarrels leading to bloodshed and ending in utter disbelief in religion, i.e. God Himself.

—Gandhi, M.K., *Harijan*, 30 January 1937.

Mr. Keithan who was here the other day was not quite sure what was at the back of Gandhiji's mind when he said that all religions were not only true but equal. Scientifically, he felt, it was hardly correct to say that all religions are equal. People would make comparisons between animists and theists. 'I would say,' said Mr. Keithan, 'it is no use comparing religions. They are different ways. Do you think we can explain the thing in different terms?'

'You are right when you say that it is impossible to compare them. But the deduction from it is that they are equal. All men are born free and equal, but one is much stronger or weaker than another physically and mentally. Therefore, superficially there is no equality between the two. But there is an essential equality. In our nakedness God is not going to think of me as Gandhi and you as Keithan. And what are we in this mighty universe? We are less than atoms, and as between atoms there is no use asking which is smaller and which is bigger. Inherently we are equal. The differences of race and skin, of mind and body, and of climate and nation are transitory. In the same way, essentially, all religions are equal. If you read the Quran, you must read it with the eye of the Muslim; if you read the Bible, you must read it with the eye of the Christian; if you read the Gita you must read it with the eye of a Hindu. Where is the use of scanning details and then holding up a religion to ridicule? Take the very first chapter of Genesis or of Matthew. We read a long pedigree and then at the end we are told Jesus was born of a virgin. You come up against a blind wall. But I must read it all with the eye of a Christian.'

'Then,' said Mr. Keithan, 'even in our Bible, there is the question of Moses and Jesus. We must hold them to be equal?'

'Yes,' said Gandhiji. 'All prophets are equal. It is a horizontal plain.'

'If we think in terms of Einstein's Relativity all are equal. But I cannot happily express the equality.'

'That is why I say they are equally true and equally imperfect. The finer the line you draw, the nearer it approaches Euclid's true straight line, but it never is the true straight line. The tree of Religion is the same, there is not that physical equality between the branches. They are all growing, and the person who belongs to the growing branch must not gloat over it and say, "Mine is the superior one." None is superior, none is inferior, to the other.'

—'Weekly Letter: Equality of Religions', *Harijan*, Vol. 5, No. 4, 13 March 1937, p. 38.

16

Hinduism's Contribution to the Civilization

Varnashrama Dharma defines man's mission on this earth. He is not born day after day to explore avenues for amassing riches and to explore different means of livelihood; on the contrary man is born in order that he may utilize every atom of his energy for his purpose of knowing his Maker. It restricts him, therefore, for the purpose of holding body and soul together, to the occupation of his forefathers. That and nothing more or nothing less is Varnashrama Dharma.

—Gandhi, M.K., *Young India*, 27 October 1927.

I consider the four divisions alone to be fundamental, natural, and essential. The innumerable sub castes are sometimes a convenience, often a hindrance. The sooner there is fusion the batter.

—Gandhi, M.K., *Young India*, 8 December 20.

Today Brahmanas and Kshatriyas, Vaishyas and Shudras are mere labels. There is utter confusion of varna as I understand it and I wish that all the Hindus will voluntarily call themselves Shudras. That is the only way to demonstrate the truth of Brahmanism and to revive

Varnadhrma in its true state.

—Gandhi, M.K., *Harijan*, 25 March 33.

I have frequently said that I do not believe in caste in the modern sense. It is an excrescence and a handicap on progress. Nor, do I believe in inequalities between human being. We are all absolutely equal. But equality is of souls and not bodies. Hence, it is a mental state. We need to think of, and to assert, equality because we see great inequalities in the physical world. We have to realize equalities in the midst of this apparent external to realize equality in the midst of this apparent external inequality. Assumption of superiority by any person over any other is a sin against god and man. Thus caste, in so far as it connotes distinctions in status, is an evil. I do, however, believe in Varna which is based on hereditary occupations, Varnas are four to mark four universal occupations—imparting knowledge, defending the defence less, carrying on agriculture and commerce, and performing service through physical labour. These occupations ate common to all mankind, but Hinduism, having recognized them as the law of our being, has made use of it in regulating social relations and conduct. Gravitation affects us all, whether one knows its existence or not. But scientist who knew the law have made it yield results that have startled the world. Even so, has Hinduism started the world by its discovery and application of the law of Varna. When Hindus were seized with inertia, abuse of Varna resulted in innumerable castes, with unnecessary and harmful restrictions to inter-dining. The law of Varna has nothing to do with these restrictions. People of different Varnas may be necessary in the interest of chastity and hygiene. But a Brahmana who marries a Shudra girl, or vice versa, commits no offence against the law of Varna.

—Gandhi, M.K., *Young India*, 4 June 31.

It is as wrong to destroy caste of the out caste, as it would be to destroy a body because of an ugly growth in it or if a crop because of the weeds. The out casteness, in the sense we understand it, has there fore to be destroyed altogether. It is an excess to be removed, if the whole system is not to perish. Untouchability is the product, there fore, not of the caste system, but of the distinction of high and low that has crept into Hinduism and is corroding it. The attack on untouchability is thus an attack upon this 'high-and-low '-ness. the moment untouchability goes, the caste system itself will be purified, that is to say, according to my dream, it will resolve itself into the true Varnadharma, the four divisions of society, each complementary of the other and none inferior or superior to any other, each as necessary for the whole body of Hinduism as any other.

—Gandhi, M.K., *Harijan*, 11 February 33.

From the economic point of view, its value was once very grate. It ensured hereditary skill; it limited competition. It was the best remedy against pauperism. And it had all the advantages of trade guilds. Although it did not foster adventure or invention there, it is not known to have come in the way either.

Historically speaking, caste may be regarded as man's experiment or social adjustment in the laboratory of Indian society. If we can prove it to be a success, it can be offered to the world as a leaven and as the nest remedy against heartless competition and social disintegration born of avarice and greed.

—Gandhi, M.K., *Young India*, 5 January 21.

Through there is in Varashrama no prohibition against inter-marriage and inter-dining, there can be no compulsion. It must be left to the unfettered choice of the individual as to where he or she will marry or dine.

—Gandhi, M.K., *Harijan*, 16 November 35.

17

The Law of Varna

Varna means pre-determination of the choice of man's profession. The law of *varna* is that a man shall follow the profession of his ancestors for earning his livelihood. *Varna* therefore is in a way the law of heredity. *Varna* is not a thing that is superimposed on Hindus, but men who were trustees for their welfare discovered the law for them. It is not a human invention, but an immutable law of nature—the statement of tendency that is ever present and at work like Newton's law of gravitation. Just as the law of gravitation existed even before it was discovered so did the law of *varna*. It was given to the Hindus to discover that law. By their discovery and application of certain laws of nature, the people of the West have easily increased their material possessions. Similarly, Hindus by their discovery of this irresistible social tendency have been able to achieve in the spiritual field what no other nation in the world has achieved.

Varna has nothing to do with caste. Down with the monster of caste that masquerades in the guise of *varna*. It is this travesty of *varna* that has degraded Hinduism and India. Our failure to follow the law of *varna* is largely responsible both for our economic and spiritual ruin. It is one cause of unemployment and impoverishment, and it is responsible for untouchability and defections from our faith.

In ages gone by there was not the ambition of encroaching on another's profession and amassing wealth. In Cicero's time, for instance, the lawyer's was an honorary profession. And it would be quite right for any brainy carpenter to become a lawyer for service, not for money. Later, ambition for fame and wealth crept in. Physicians served the society and rested content with what it gave them, but now they have become traders and even a danger to society. The medical and the legal professions were deservedly called liberal when the motive was purely philanthropic.

—Gandhi, M.K., *Young India*, 24 November 1927, pp. 390, 391–95.

Varnashrama, as I interpret it, satisfies the religious, social and economic needs of a community. It satisfies the religious needs, because a whole community accepting the law is free to devote ample time to spiritual perfection. Observance of the law obviates social evils and entirely prevents the killing economic competition. And if it is regarded as a law laying down, not the rights or the privileges of the community governed by it, but their duties, it ensures the fairest possible distribution of wealth, though it may not be an ideal, i.e. strictly equal, distribution. Therefore, when people in disregard of the law mistake duties for privileges and try to pick and choose occupations for self-advancement, it leads to confusion of *varna* and ultimate disruption of society.

—Gandhi, M.K., *Harijan*, 4 March 1938, p. 5.

18

Shortcomings of Hinduism

I have always claimed to be a Sanatani Hindu. It is not that I am quite innocent of the scriptures. I am not a profound scholar of Sanskrit. I have read the Vedas and the Upanishads only in translation. Naturally therefore mine is not a scholarly study of them. My knowledge of them is in no way profound, but I have studied them as I should do as a Hindu and I claim to have grasped their true spirit. By the time I had reached the age of 21, I had studied other religions also.

There was a time when I was wavering between Hinduism and Christianity. When I recovered my balance of mind, I felt that to me salvation was possible only through the Hindu religion and my faith in Hinduism grew deeper and more enlightened.

But even then I believed that untouchability was no part of Hinduism; and that, if it was, such Hinduism was not for me.

True, Hinduism does not regard untouchability as a sin. I do not want to enter into any controversy regarding the interpretation of the shastras. It might be difficult for me to establish my point by quoting authorities from the Bhagwata or the Manusmriti. But I claim to have understood the spirit of Hinduism. Hinduism has sinned in giving sanction to untouchability. It has degraded us, made us the pariahs, of the Empire. Even the Mussulmans caught the sinful contagion from us, and in South Africa, in East Africa and in Canada the Mussulmans no less than the Hindus came to be regarded as pariahs. All this evil has resulted from the sin of untouchability.

—Gandhi, M.K., *Young India*, 27 April 1921, p. 135

Untouchability is not a sanction of religion, it is a device of Satan. The devil has always quoted scriptures. But scriptures cannot transcend reason and truth. They are intended to purify reason and illuminate truth. I am not going to burn a spotless horse because the Vedas are reported to have advised, tolerated, or sanctioned the sacrifice. For me the Vedas are divine and unwritten. 'The letter killeth.' It is the spirit that giveth the light. And the spirit of the Vedas is purity, truth, innocence, chastity, humility, simplicity, forgiveness, godliness, and all that makes a man or woman noble and brave. There is neither nobility nor bravery in treating the great and uncomplaining scavengers of the nation as worse than dogs to be despised and spat upon.

—Quoted in Desai, Mahadev, 'The Week: Conversion', *Young India*, Vol. 10, No. 1, 19 January 1928, p. 22.

...I think we are committing a great sin in treating a whole class of people as untouchables and it is owing to the existence of this class that we have still some revolting practices among us. Not to eat in company with a particular person and not to touch him are two very different things. No one is an untouchable now. If we don't mind contact with a Christian or a Muslim, why should we mind it with one belonging to our own religion? No defence of untouchability is possible now, either from the point of view of justice or that of practical common sense.

—Gandhi, M.K., 'Fragment Of Letter To Mathuradas Trikumji', *The Collected Works of Mahatma Gandhi (Electronic Book)*, Vol. XV, Publications Division Government of India, New Delhi, 1999.

I do not want to be reborn. But if I have to be reborn, I should be born an untouchable, so that I may share their sorrows, sufferings, and the affronts leveled at them, in order that I may endeavour to free myself and them from that miserable condition. I, therefore, prayed that, if I should be born again, I should do so not as a Brahmin, Kshatriya, Vaishya or Shudra, but as an Atishudra.

—'Mr Gandhi and the Suppressed Classes', *Young India*, Vol. 3, No. 18, 4 May 1921, p. 144.

'...I was wedded to the work for the extinction of "untouchability" long before I was wedded to my wife. There were two occasions in our joint life when there was choice between working for the untouchables and remaining with my wife and I would have preferred the first. But thanks to my good wife, the crisis was averted. In my Ashram, which is my family, I have several *Untouchables* and a sweet but naughty girl living as my own daughter.'

—Quoted in Desai, Mahadev, 'The Birmingham Visit: The Meeting', *Young India*, Vol. 13, No. 45, 5 November 1931, p. 341.

Love of the people brought the problem of untouchability early into my life. My mother said, 'You must not touch this boy, he is an untouchable.' 'Why not?' I questioned back, and from that day my revolt began.

—Gandhi, M.K., *Harijan*, 24 December 1938, p. 393.

Swaraj is a meaningless term, if we desire to keep a fifth of India under perpetual subjection, and deliberately deny to them the fruits of national culture. We are seeking the aid of God in this great purifying movement, but we deny to the most deserving among his creatures the rights of humanity. Inhuman ourselves we may not plead before the Throne for deliverance from the inhumanity of others.

—Gandhi, M.K., 'The Simla Visit', *Young India*, Vol. 3, No. 18, 25 May 1921, p. 165.

In these days of self-purification, Harijans ought to know that they are to avoid all the bad customs of caste-Hindus. They should therefore avoid child marriages. But reformers may not be impatient. Sarda Act is, in my opinion, a wise step. But it may not be strictly enforced against Harijans when it is very laxly enforced against caste-Hindus. There should be effective enlightened propaganda by Harijans among fellow Harijans on the evil of child marriages and the bearing of the Sarda Act on them. And then when it is made certain that people willfully ignore that Act a few prosecutions may be undertaken. But even then, they must be the sole concern of Harijans. They may not ask for or receive even financial assistance in this matter from caste-Hindus. In any case at least one year should be given to concentrated propaganda.

—Gandhi, M.K., *Letters To Rajkumari Amrit Kaur*, Navajivan Publishing House, 1961, p. 11.

Castes are innumerable and in their present condition they are a drag upon Hinduism... *Varna* stands on a different footing, and it means profession. It has nothing to do with inter-dining and inter-marriage. People belonging to the four professions used formerly to inter-dine and even to intermarry and by so doing they naturally could not and did not leave their *varna*. This is absolutely clear from the definitions of the different *varnas* in the Bhagavadgita. A man falls from his varna when he abandons his hereditary profession. Today however *varnashram* is a lost treasure and there is utter confusion.

—Gandhi, M.K., *Selected Letters: Second Series*, Valji Govindji Desai (trans.), Navajivan Publishing House, 1962.

19

On Women's Status

Of all the evils for which man has made himself responsible, none is so degrading, so shocking or so brutal as his abuse of the better half of humanity to me, the female sex, not the weaker sex. It is the nobler of the two, for it is even today the embodiment of sacrifice, silent suffering, humility, faith and knowledge.

—Gandhi, M.K., 'Our Fallen Sisters', *Young India*, Vol. 3, No. 35, 15 September 1921, p. 292.

To call woman the weaker sex is a libel; it is man's injustice to woman. If by strength is meant brute strength, then, indeed, is woman less brute than man. If by strength is meant moral power, then woman is immeasurably man's superior. Has she not greater intuition, is she not more self-sacrificing, has she not greater courage? Without her man could not be. If non-violence is the law of our being, the future is with woman... Who can make a more effective appeal to the heart than woman?

—Gandhi, M.K., *Young India*, 10 April 1930, p. 121.

If I was born a woman, I would rise in rebellion against any pretension on the part of man that woman is born to be his plaything. I have mentally become a woman in order to steal into her heart. I could not steal into my wife's heart until I decided to treat her differently than I used to do, and so I restored to her all her rights by dispossessing myself of all my so-called rights as her husband. And you see her today as simple as myself.

You find no necklaces, no fineries on her. I want you to be like that. Refuse to be the slaves of your own whims and fancies, and the slaves of men. Refuse to decorate yourselves, and don't go in for scents and lavender waters; if you [woman] want to give out the proper scent, it must come out of your heart, and then you will captivate not man, but humanity. It is your birth-right. Man is born of woman, he is flesh of her flesh and bone of her bone. Come to your own and deliver your message again.

—Gandhi, M.K., *Young India*, 8 December 1927, p. 406.

Had not man in his blind selfishness crushed woman's soul as he has done or had she not succumbed to 'the enjoyments' she would have given the world an exhibition of the infinite strength that is latent in her. The world shall see it in all its wonder and glory when woman has secured an equal opportunity for herself with man and fully developed her powers of mutual aid and combination.

—Gandhi, M.K., *Young India*, 7 May 1931, p. 96.

Woman, I hold, is the personification of self-sacrifice, but unfortunately today she does not realize what a tremendous advantage she has over man. As Tolstoy used to say, they are labouring under the hypnotic influence of man. If they would realize the strength of non-violence they would not consent to be called the weaker sex.

—Gandhi, M.K., *Young India*, 14 January 1932, p. 19.

Man has regarded woman as his tool. She has learnt to be his tool, and in the end found it easy and pleasurable to be such because when one drags another in his fall the descent is easy.

—Gandhi, M.K., *Harijan*, 25 January 1936, p. 396.

Woman has circumvented man in a variety of ways in her unconsciously subtle ways, as man has vainly and equally unconsciously struggled to thwart woman in gaining ascendancy over him. The result is a stalemate. Thus viewed, it is a serious problem the enlightened daughters of Bharat Mata are called upon to solve. They may not ape the manner of the West, which may be suited to its environment. They must apply methods suited to the Indian genius and Indian environment. Theirs must be the strong, controlling, purifying, steadying hand, conserving what is best in our culture and unhesitatingly rejecting what is base and degrading. This is the work of Sitas, Draupadis, Savitris, and Damayantis, not of amazons and prudes.

—Gandhi, M.K., *Young India*, 17 October 1929, p. 340.

Our women do not let male doctors to examine their bodies or to operate upon them. This is a false sense of modesty which has its root in sex-obsession. In this matter I prefer the practice of the West. I do know that at times undesirable consequences have resulted from it. When unscrupulous doctors and women who are easily duped or roused to passion come together, it has led to immoral acts. But that kind of thing happens in this world practically under any other set of circumstances, and there is no reason why on that account necessary and good activities should be put to a stop. We must have confidence in ourselves.

—Naryan, Shriman (ed.),
The Selected Works Of Mahatma Gandhi 5, Navajivan Publishing House, 1968, pp, 425–26.

It is the lust of men which has often degraded women and taught them ways of dressing and behaving, whereby women might tempt and excite them. The woman did not see this in the sense of her own enslavement and degradation. She also harboured lust, and so she bored her nose, bored her ears and put on shackles (in the form of ornaments) on her feet and became a slave. An unscrupulous man can easily tempt a woman with a nose-ring or earring. I have never been able to understand why women put on these things which lead to their disablement. Real beauty lies in the heart.

—Gandhi, M.K., *The Selected Works Of Mahatma Gandhi Vol. 5*, Shriman Narayan (ed.), Navajivan Publishing House, 1968, p. 426.

Chastity cannot be protected by the surrounding wall of the Purdah. It must grow from within and it must be capable of withstanding every unsought temptation.

—Gandhi, M.K., *Young India*, 3 February 1927.

Why is there all this morbid anxiety about female purity? Have women any say in the matter of male purity? Female or male purity cannot be superimposed from without. It is a matter of evolution from within and therefore of individual self-effort.

—Gandhi, M.K., *Young India*, 25 November 1926.

Women must not suffer any legal disability which is not suffered by men. Both are perfectly equal.

—Gandhi, M.K., *Young India*, 17 October 1929.

Sexual equality does not translate into occupational equality in spite of the absence of a legal bar. Women instinctively recoil from a function that belongs to men. Nature has created sexes as complements of each other. Their functions are defined as are their forms.

—Gandhi, M.K., *Harijan*, 2 December 1939.

The dowry system is a product of the caste system. The abolition of caste will lead to the abolition of dowry.

—Gandhi, M.K., *Harijan*, 23 May 1936.

Demanding dowry is akin to discrediting womanhood. Young men who demand dowry should be excommunicated. Parents of girls should cease to be dazzled by English degrees and should not hesitate to travel outside their little castes and provinces to secure true, gallant young men for their daughters.

—Gandhi, M.K., *Young India*, 21 June 1928.

Marriage confers no right upon one partner to demand obedience of the other. However, divorce is not the only alternative. Marriage is a state of discipline. When one partner breaks discipline, the other can break the bond.

The breach here is moral and not physical. It precludes divorce. Hinduism regards each as absolute equal of the other. Hinduism leaves the individual absolutely free for the sake of self-realization, for which and which alone he or she is born.

—Gandhi, M.K., *Young India*, 21 October 1926.

Education enables women to uphold their natural rights. Men and women are complementary to each other. Man is supreme in the outward activities and therefore he should have a greater knowledge thereof. Home life is entirely the sphere of woman and therefore in domestic affairs, in the upbringing and education of children women ought to have more knowledge. Unless courses of instruction are based on a discriminating appreciation of these basic principles, the fullest life of man and woman cannot be developed.

—Gandhi, M.K., *Harijan*, 27 February 1937.

20

My Views on Untouchability

My views on untouchability are not the product of my Western education. I had formed them long before I went to England, and long before I studied the scriptures, and in an atmosphere which was by no means favourable to those views. For I was born in an orthodox Vaishnava family and yet ever since I reached the year of discretion I have firmly held my uncompromising views in the matter, which later comparative study of Hinduism and experience have only confirmed. How in face of the fact that no scriptural text mentions a fifth varna, and in face of the express injunction of the Gita to regard a brahmana and a bhangi as equals, we persist in maintaining this deep blot on Hinduism, I cannot understand. Regarding a brahmana and a bhangi as equals does not mean that you will not accord to a true brahmana the reverence that is due to him, but that the brahmana and the bhangi are equally entitled to our service, that we accord to the bhangi the same rights of sending his children to public schools, of visiting public temples, of the use of public wells, etc., on the same basis as these rights are enjoyed by any other Hindu.

—Gandhi, M.K., 'Speech on Untouchability, Akola, February 6, 1927', *Young India*, 17 February 1927.

It is my certain conviction that, if the Hindu heart is completely purged of the taint of untouchability, the event will have its inevitable influence not only upon all the communities in India but on the whole world. This belief is daily becoming stronger. I cannot remove from my heart untouchability regarding several millions of human beings and harbour it towards some other millions. The very act of the Hindu heart getting rid of distinctions of high and low must cure us of mutual jealousies and distrust of and among other communities. It is for that reason that I have staked my life on this issue. In fighting this battle against untouchability, I am fighting for unity not only among Hindu 'touchables' and Hindu 'untouchables' but among Hindus, Muslims, Christians and all other different religious communities.

—Gandhi, M.K., *Harijan*, 17 November 1933, p. 4.

There should be not only no untouchability as between Hindus and Hindus, but there should be no untouchability whatsoever between Hindus, Christians, Mussalmans, Parsis and the rest. I am convinced that if this great change of heart can be brought about, we should live in India as one people trusting each other and without any mutual distrust or suspicion. It is untouchability with all its subtle forms that separates us from one another and makes life itself unlovely and difficult to live.

—Gandhi, M.K., *Harijan*, 26 January 34, p. 4.

Removal of untouchability means love for, and service of, the whole world, and thus merges into Ahimsa. Removal of untouchability spells the breaking down of barriers between man and man, and between the various orders of Being. We find such barriers erected everywhere in the world.

—Gandhi, M.K., *From Yeravda Mandir: Ashram Observances*, Valji Govindji Desai (trans.), Navajivan Publishing House, 1933, pp. 33–34.

21

My Case against Untouchability

The readers will recall the fact that Dr. Ambedkar was to have presided last May at the annual conference of the Jat-Pat-Torak Mandal of Lahore. But the conference itself was cancelled because Dr. Ambedkar's address was found by the Reception Committee to be unacceptable...

Dr. Ambedkar was not going to be beaten by the Reception Committee. He has answered their rejection of him by publishing the address at his own expense. He has priced it at 8 annas. I would suggest a reduction to 2 annas or at least 4 annas.

No reformer can ignore the address. The orthodox will gain by reading it. This is not to say that the address is not open to objection. It has to be read if only because it is open to serious objection. Dr. Ambedkar is a challenge to Hinduism. Brought up as a Hindu, educated by a Hindu potentate, he has become so disgusted with the so-called Savarna Hindus for the treatment that he and his have received at their hands that he proposes to leave not only them but the very religion that is his and their common heritage. He has transferred to that religion his disgust against a part of its professors.

But this is not to be wondered at. After all one can only judge a system or an institution by the conduct of its representatives. What is more, Dr. Ambedkar found that the vast majority of Savarna Hindus had not only conducted themselves inhumanly against those of their fellow religionists whom they classed as untouchables, but they had based their conduct on the authority of their scriptures, and when he began to search, them he had found ample warrant for their belief in untouchability and all its implications. The author of the address has quoted chapter and verse in proof of his threefold indictment—inhuman conduct itself, the unabashed justification for it on the part of the perpetrators, and the subsequent discovery that the justification was warranted by their scriptures.

—Gandhi, M.K., 'Dr Ambedkar's Indictment',
Harijan, Vol. 4, No. 22, 11 July 1936.

The stories told in the Puranas are some of them most dangerous, if we do not know their bearing on the present conditions. The shastras would be death-traps if we were to regulate our conduct according to every detail given in them or according to that of the characters therein described. They help us only to define and argue out fundamental principles. If some well-known character in religious books sinned against God or man, is that a warrant for our repeating the sin? It is enough for us to be told, once for all, that Truth is the only thing that matters in the world, that Truth is God. It is irrelevant to be told that even Yudhishthira was betrayed into an untruth. It is more relevant/for us to know that when he spoke an untruth, he had to suffer for it that very moment and that his great name in no way protected him from punishment. Similary, it is irrelevant for us to be told that Adishankara avoided a *Chandala*. It is enough for us to know that a religion that teaches us to treat all that lives as we treat ourselves, cannot possibly countenance the inhuman treatment of a single creature, let alone a whole class of perfectly innocent human beings. Moreover we have not even all the facts before us to judge what Adishankara did or did not do. Still less, do we know the meaning of the word chandala where it occurs. It has admittedly many meanings, one of which is a sinner. But if all sinners are to be regarded as untouchables, it is very much to be feared that we should all, not excluding the Pandit himself, be under the ban of untouchability. That untouchability is an old institution, nobody has ever denied. But, if it is an evil, it cannot be defended on the ground of its antiquity.

—Gandhi, M.K., 'Hydra-Headed Monster', *Young India*, Vol. 8, No. 30, 29 July 1926, p. 268.

22

Defending Tulsidas's Ramayana

Several friends on various occasions have addressed to me criticisms regarding my attitude towards the Tulsi-Ramayan. The substance of their criticisms is as follows:

> You have described the Ramayan as the best, of books, but we have never been able to reconcile ourselves with your view. Do not you see how Tulsidas has disparaged womankind, defended Rama's unchivalrous ambuscade on Vali, praised Vibhishan for betrayal of his country, and described Rama as an avatara in spite of his gross injustice to Sita? What beauty do you find in a book like this? Or do you think that the poetic beauty of the book compensates for everything else? If it is so then we venture to suggest that you have no qualifications for the task.

I admit that if we take the criticisms of every point individually they will be found difficult to refute and the whole of the Ramayan can, in this manner, be easily condemned. But that can be said of almost everything and everybody. There is a story related about a celebrated artist that in order to answer his critics he put his picture in a show window and invited visitors to indicate their opinion by marking the spot they did not like. The result was that there was hardly any portion that was not covered by the critics' marks. As a matter of fact, however, the picture was a masterpiece of art. Indeed even the Vedas, the Bible and the Quran have not been exempt from condemnation. In order to arrive at a proper estimate of a book it must be judged as a whole. So much for external criticism. The internal test of a book consists in finding out what effect it has produced on the majority of its readers. Judged by either method the position of the Ramayan as a book par excellence remains unassailable. This, however, does not mean that it is absolutely faultless. But it is claimed on behalf of the Ramayan that it has given peace to millions, has given faith to those who had it not, and is even today serving as a healing balm to thousands who are burnt by the fire of unbelief. Every page of it is overflowing with devotion. It is a veritable mine of spiritual experience.

It is true that the Ramayan is sometimes used by evil-minded persons to support their evil practices. But that is no proof of evil in the Ramayan. I admit that Tulsidas has, unintentionally as I think, done injustice to womankind. In this, as in several other respects also, he has failed to rise above the prevailing notions of his age. In other words Tulsidas was not a reformer; he was only a prince among devotees. The faults of the Ramayan are less a reflection on Tulsidas than a reflection on the age in which he lived.

What should be the attitude of the reformer regarding the position of women or towards Tulsidas under such circumstances? Can he derive no help whatever from Tulsidas? The reply is emphatically 'he can'. In spite of disparaging remarks about women in the Ramayan it should not be forgotten that in it Tulsidas has presented to the world his matchless picture of Sita. Where would Rama be without Sita? We find a host of other ennobling figures like Kausalya, Sumitra etc. in the Ramayan. We bow our head in reverence before the faith and devotion of Shabari and Ahalya. Ravana was a monster but Mandodari was a sati. In my opinion these instances go to prove that Tulsidas was no reviler of women by conviction. On the contrary, so far as his convictions went, he had only reverence for them. So much for Tulsidas's attitude towards women.

In the matter of the killing of Vali, however, there is room for two opinions. In Vibhishan I can find no fault. Vibhishan offered Satyagraha against his brother. His example teaches us that it is a travesty of patriotism to sympathize with or try to conceal the faults of one's rulers or country, and to oppose them is the truest patriotism. By helping Rama Vibhishan rendered the truest service to his country. The treatment of Sita by Rama does not denote heartlessness. It is a proof of a duel between kingly duty and a husband's love for wife.

To the sceptics who feel honest doubts in connection with the Ramayan, I would suggest that they should not accept anybody's interpretations mechanically. They should leave out such portions about which they feel doubtful. Nothing contrary to truth and ahimsa need be condoned. It would be sheer perversity to argue that because in our opinion Rama practised deception, we too may do likewise. The proper thing to do would be to believe that Rama was incapable of practising deception. As the Gita says, 'There is nothing in the world that is entirely free from fault.' Let us, therefore, like the fabled swan who rejects the water and takes only the milk, learn to treasure only the good and reject the evil in everything. Nothing and no one is perfect but God.

—Gandhi, M.K., 'Tulsidas', *Young India*, Vol. 11, No. 44, 31 October 1929.

23

Satan in Hinduism

A correspondent writes:

> A few months back under a heading not quite justified by its contents you published a letter of mine concerning certain religious systems and the belief in God. Now I am tempted to put you a question concerning his adversary (according to Semitic beliefs), whose name you are so often using in your writings and speeches—not of course without effect, as witness the article 'Snares of Satan' in your issue of 6 August 1925. If it was only rhetorical effect that was intended thereby because you were writing or speaking in the language of a people who have been taught to believe in Satan's existence through the Semitic creed of Christianity, then I would have nothing to say. But the article cited, among other things, does seem to point to a belief on your part in Satan's existence,—a belief, in my humble opinion, quite un-Hindu.
>
> Asked by Arjuna what was the cause of man's continual fall, Sri Krishna said: 'Kama esha, krodha esha (It is lust, it is anger)'. According to Hindu belief, it would seem, the Tempter is no person

outside of us, nor indeed is it one; for there are the six enemies' of man enumerated in the Shastras: kama or lust, krodha or anger, lobha or greed, moha or infatuation, mada or pride, and matsara, i.e., envy or jealousy. So it is clear, Hinduism has no place for Satan, the Fallen Angel, the Tempter, or as he has been called by a French writer (Anatole France), 'God's man-of-affairs'! How is it then that you who are a Hindu speak and write as if you believed in the real existence of the Old One?

This correspondent is well known to the readers of *Young India*. He is too wide awake not to know the sense in which I could use the word Satan. But I have observed in him a disposition to draw me out on many matters about which there is a likelihood of the slightest misunderstanding or about which a greater elucidation may be considered necessary. In my opinion the beauty of Hinduism lies in its all-embracing inclusiveness. What the divine author of the Mahabharata said of his great creation is equally true of Hinduism. What of substance is contained in any other religion is always to be found in Hinduism. And what is not contained in it is insubstantial or unnecessary. I do believe that there is room for Satan in Hinduism. The Biblical conception is neither new nor original. Satan is not a personality even in the Bible. Or he is as much a personality in the Bible as Ravana or the whole brood of the Asuras is in Hinduism. I no more believe in a historical Ravana with ten heads and twenty arms than in a historical Satan. And even as Satan and his companions are fallen angels, so are Ravana and his companions fallen angels or call them gods, if you will. If it be a crime to clothe evil passions and ennobling thoughts in personalities, it is a crime for which perhaps Hinduism is the most responsible. For are not the six passions referred to by my correspondent, and nameless others, embodied in Hinduism? Who or what is Dhritarashtra and his hundred sons? To the end of time imagination, that is, poetry, will play a useful and necessary part in the human evolution. We shall continue to talk of passions as if they were persons. Do they not torment us as much as evil persons? Therefore, as in innumerable other things, in the matter under notice the letter killeth, the spirit giveth life.

—Gandhi, M.K., *Young India*, 17 September 1925, p. 32.

24

The Ethical Religion of Higher Morality

It is sometimes said that all morality involves social relations. This is well said; for instance, if the judge has a proper sense of justice, men who go to court obtain satisfaction. Similarly love, kindness, generosity and other qualities can be manifested only in relation to others. The force of loyalty can be demonstrated only in our relations with one another. Of patriotism, nothing need be said. Truly speaking, there is no aspect of morality the benefit of which accrues to the practitioner alone. Sometimes it is said that truthfulness and other virtues have nothing to do with the other person and are entirely personal. But we must admit that by telling the truth we prevent harm to another we do him an injury.

In the same way, when a man disapproves of certain laws or customs and withdraws from society, even then his acts affect society. Such a man lives in a world of ideals. He does not worry that the world of his ideals is not yet born. From him the mere thought that the prevailing standard is not good enough is sufficient to impel him to resist it. He will constantly try to change other people's way of life to his own. This is how prophets have caused the world's wheels to change their course.

So long as man remains selfish and does not care for

the happiness of others, he is no better than an animal and perhaps worse. His superiority to the animal is seen only when we find him caring for his family. He is still more human, that is, much higher than the animal, when he extends his concept of the family to include his country or community as well. He climbs still higher in the scale when he comes to regard the human race as his family. A man is an animal or imperfect [as a human being] to the extent that he falls behind in his service to humanity. If I feel my wife's injury or that of my community, yet have no sympathy for anyone outside the circle, it is clear that I do not have any feeling for humanity as such; but I have, simply out of selfishness or a sense of discrimination, a certain feeling for my wife, my children or the community which I hold as my own.

That is to say, we have neither practiced nor known ethical religion so long as we do not feel sympathy for every human being. Now we know that the higher morality must be comprehensive; it must embrace all men. Considering our relation to mankind, every man has a claim over us, as it our duty always to serve him. We should act on the assumption that we have no claim on others. He is merely ignorant who would here argue that the man acting in this manner will be trampled in the world's scramble. For it is a universal experience that God always saves the man who whole-heartedly devotes himself the service of others.

According to this moral standard all men are equal. This is not to be interpreted to mean equality of position and function for all. It only means that, if I hold a high place, I also have the ability to shoulder its duties and responsibilities. I should not therefore lose my head and believe that men with smaller responsibilities are my inferiors. Equality depends on the state of our mind, and until our mind reaches that state, we shall remain backward.

According to this moral standard no nation can rule another for selfish ends. It is immoral of the American people to reduce the aborigines to an inferior status and run the government. A civilized race coming into contact with a savage one owes it to the latter to raise it to its own level. The same standard rules that the king is the servant and not the master of his people and that officers are not there to enjoy power but to make the people happy. If the people in a democratic State are selfish, that State comes to no good.

Moreover, according to this law, the stronger members of a State or community have to protect, not oppress, the weaker ones. Under such a government there can be no starvation; nor can there be happy while we see our neighbors languishing in misery. The man following this high moral standard will never amass wealth. He who would be moral need not be scared away by the thought that few follow this ideal morality; for he is master of his morality, not of its results. He will be considered guilty if he does not practice morality; but nobody will find fault with him if his immoral behaviour has no consequence for society.

—Gandhi, M.K., *Ethical Religion*, Navajivan Publishing House, Ahmedabad, 1968.

25

The Hindu-Muslim Feud

In my opinion there is no such thing as proselytism in Hinduism as it is understood in Christianity or to a lesser extent in Islam. The Arya Samaj has, I think, copied the Christians in planning its propaganda. The modern method does not appeal to me. It has done more harm than good.

Though regarded as a matter of the heart purely and one between the Maker and oneself, it has degenerated into an appeal to the selfish instinct. The Arya Samaj preacher is never so happy as when he is reviling other religions. My Hindu instinct tells me that all religions are more or less true.

All proceed from the same God, but all are imperfect human instrumentality. The real shuddhi movement should consist in each one trying to arrive at perfection in his or her own faith. In such a plan character would be the only test. What is the use of crossing from one compartment to another, if it does not mean a moral rise? What is the meaning of my trying to convert to the service of God (for that must be the implication of shuddhi or tabligh) when those who are in my fold are every day denying God by their actions?

'Physician, heal thyself' is more true in matters religious

than mundane. But these are my views. If the Arya Samajists think that they have a call from their conscience, they have a perfect right to conduct the movement. Such a burning call recognizes no time limit, no checks of experience.

If Hindu-Muslim unity is endangered because an Arya Samaj preacher or a Mussulman preacher preaches his faith in obedience to a call from within, that unity is only skin-deep. Why should we be ruffled by such movements? Only they must be genuine. If the Malkanas wanted to return to the Hindu fold, they had a perfect right to do so whenever they liked.

But no propaganda can be allowed which reviles other religions. For that would be negation of toleration. The best way of dealing with such propaganda is to publicly condemn it.

—Gandhi, M.K., *Young India*,
23 April 1931.

26

Die without Killing

Though the majority of the Mussulmans of India and the Hindus belong to the same 'stock', the religious environment has made them different. I believe and I have noticed too that thought transforms man's features as well as character. The Sikhs are the most recent illustration of the fact.

The Mussulman being generally in a minority has as a class developed into a bully. Moreover, being heir to fresh traditions he exhibits the virility of a comparatively new system of life. Though in my opinion non-violence has a predominant place in the Quran, the thirteen hundred years of imperialistic expansion has made the Mussulmans fighters as a body. They are therefore aggressive.

Bullying is the natural excrescence of an aggressive spirit. The Hindu has an ages-old civilization. He is essentially non-violent. His civilization has passed through the experiences that the two recent ones are still passing through. If Hinduism was ever imperialistic in the modern sense of the term, it has outlived its imperialism and has either deliberately or as a matter of course given it up.

Pre-dominance of the non-violent spirit has restricted the use of arms to a small minority which must always be subordinate to a civil power highly spiritual, learned and selfless. The Hindus as a body are therefore not equipped for fighting.

But not having retained their spiritual training, they have forgotten the use of an effective substitute for arms, and not knowing their use nor having an aptitude for them, they have become docile to the point of timidity or cowardice. This vice is therefore a natural excrescence of gentleness. Holding this view, I do not think that the Hindu exclusiveness, bad as it undoubtedly is, has much to do with the Hindu timidity.

Hence also my disbelief in *akhadas* as a means of self-defence. I prize them for physical culture but, for self-defence, I would restore the spiritual culture. The best and most lasting self-defence is self-purification. I refuse to be lifted off my feet because of the scares that haunt us today.

If Hindus would but believe in themselves and work in accordance with their traditions, they will have no reason to fear bullying. The moment they recommence the real spiritual training the Mussulman will respond. He cannot help it. If I can get together a band of young Hindus with faith in themselves and therefore faith in the Mussulmans, the band will become a shield for the weaker ones.

They (the young Hindus) will teach how to die without killing. I know no other way. When our ancestors saw affliction surrounding them, they went in for tapasya— purification. They realized the helplessness of the flesh and in their helplessness they prayed till they compelled the Maker to obey their call.

'O yes,' says my Hindu friend, 'but then God sent someone to weild arms.' I am not concerned with denying the truth of the retort. All I say to the friend is that as a Hindu he may not ignore the cause and secure the result. It will be time to fight when we have done enough tapasya. Are we purified enough?

—Gandhi, M.K., *Young India*,
19 June 1924.

27

Himsa in the Gita

A friend puts forward the following poser:

> The controversy about the teaching of the Gita—whether it is himsa (violence) or ahimsa (non-violence)—will, it seems, go on for a long time. It is one thing what meaning we read in the Gita, or rather we want to read in the Gita; it is another what meaning is furnished by an unbiased reading of it.

The question, therefore, does not present much difficulty to one who implicitly accepts ahimsa as the eternal principle of life. He will say that the Gita is acceptable to him only if it teaches ahimsa. A grand book like the Gita could, for him, inculcate nothing grander than the eternal religious principle of ahimsa.

If it did not it would cease to be his unerring guide. It would still be worthy of his high regard, but not an infallible authority. In the first chapter we find Arjuna laying down his weapons, under the influence of ahimsa, and ready to die at the hands of the Kauravas. He conjures up a vision of the disaster and the sin involved in himsa. He is overcome with ennui and in fear and trembling exclaims: 'Oh what a mighty sin we are up to!'

Shri Krishna catches him in that mood and tells him:

'Enough of this high philosophy; No one kills or is killed. The soul is immortal and the body must perish. Fight then the fight that has come to thee as a matter of duty. Victory or defeat is no concern of thine. Acquit thyself of thy task.' In the eleventh chapter the Lord presents a panoramic vision of the Universe and says: 'I am Kala, the Destroyer of the worlds, the Ancient of Days; I am here engaged in My task of destruction of the worlds. Kill thou those already killed by Me. Give not thyself up to grief.'

Himsa and ahimsa are equal before God. But for man what is God's message? Is it this: 'Fight; for thou art sure to foil thy enemies in the field'? If the Gita teaches ahimsa the first and the eleventh chapters are not consistent with the rest, at any rate do not support the ahimsa theory. I wish you could find time to resolve my doubt. The question put is eternal and every one who has studied the Gita must need to find out his own solution. And although I am going to offer mine, I know that ultimately one is guided not by the intellect but by the heart.

The heart accepts a conclusion for which the intellect subsequently finds the reasoning. Argument follows conviction. Man often finds reasons in support of whatever he does or wants to do. I shall therefore appreciate the position of those who are unable to accept my interpretation of the Gita. All I need do is to indicate how I reached my meaning, and what canons of interpretation I have followed in arriving at it. Mine is but to fight for my meaning, no matter whether I win or lose.

My first acquaintance with the Gita was in 1889, when I was almost twenty. I had not then much of an inkling of the principle of ahimsa. One of the lines of the Gujarati poet,

Shamal Bhatta, had taught me the principle of winning even the enemy with love, and that teaching had gone deep into me. But I had not deduced the eternal principle of non-violence from it. It did not, for instance, cover all animal life. I had, before this, tasted meat whilst in India. I thought it a duty to kill venomous reptiles like the snake.

It is my conviction today that even venomous creatures may not be killed by a believer in ahimsa. I believed in those days in preparing ourselves for a fight with the English. I often repeated a Gujarati poet's famous doggerel: 'What wonder if Britain rules!' etc. My meat-eating was as a first step to qualify myself for the fight with the English. Such was my position before I proceeded to England, and there I escaped meat-eating etc. because of my determination to follow unto death the promises I had given to my mother. My love for truth has saved me from many a pitfall.

Now whilst in England my contact with two English friends made me read the Gita. I say 'made me read', because it was not of my own desire that I read it. But when these two friends asked me to read the Gita with them, I was ashamed of my ignorance. The knowledge of my total ignorance of my scriptures pained me. Pride, I think, was at the bottom of this feeling. My knowledge of Sanskrit was not enough to enable me to understand all the verses of the Gita unaided. The friends, of course, were quite innocent of Sanskrit. They placed before me Sir Edwin Arnold's magnificent rendering of the Gita.

I devoured the contents from cover to cover and was entranced by it. The last nineteen verses of the second chapter have since been inscribed on the tablet of my heart. They contain for me all knowledge. The truths they teach are the 'eternal verities'. There is reasoning in them but they represent realized knowledge.

I have since read many translations and many commentaries, have argued and reasoned to my heart's content but the impression that the first reading gave me has never been effaced. Those verses are the key to the interpretation of the Gita. I would even advise rejection of the verses that may seem to be in conflict with them. But a humble student need reject nothing. He will simply say: 'It is the limitation of my own intellect that I cannot resolve this inconsistency. I might be able to do so in the time to come.' That is how he will plead with himself and with others.

A prayerful study and experience are essential for a correct interpretation of the scriptures. The injunction that a shudra may not study the scriptures is not entirely without meaning. A shudra means a spiritually uncultured, ignorant man. He is more likely than not to misinterpret the Vedas and other scriptures. Every one cannot solve an algebraical equation. Some preliminary study is a sine qua non. How ill would the grand truth 'I am Brahman' lie in the mouth of a man steeped in sin! To what ignoble purposes would he turn it! What a distortion it would suffer at his hands!

A man therefore who would interpret the scriptures must have the spiritual discipline. He must practise the yamas and niyamas—the eternal guides of conduct. A superficial practice thereof is useless. The shastras have enjoined the necessity of a guru. But a guru being rare in these days, a study of modern books inculcating bhakti has been suggested by the sages. Those who are lacking in bhakti, lacking in faith, are ill-qualified to interpret the scriptures. The learned may draw an elaborately learned interpretation out of them, but that will not be the true interpretation. Only the experienced will arrive at the true interpretation of the scriptures.

But even for the inexperienced there are certain canons. That interpretation is not true which conflicts with Truth. To one who doubts even Truth, the scriptures have no meaning. No one can contend with him. There is danger for the man who has failed to find ahimsa in the scriptures, but he is not doomed. Truth—Sat— is positive; non-violence is negative. Truth stands for the fact, non-violence negatives the fact. And yet nonviolence is the highest religion. Truth is self-evident; non-violence is its maturest fruit. It is contained in Truth, but as it is not self-evident a man may seek to interpret the shastras, without accepting it. But his acceptance of Truth is sure to lead him to the acceptance of non-violence.

Renunciation of the flesh is essential for realizing Truth. The sage who realized Truth found non-violence out of the violence raging all about him and said: Violence is unreal, non-violence is real. Realization of Truth is impossible without non-violence. Brahmacharya (celibacy), asteya (non-stealing), aparigraha (non-possession) are means to achieve ahimsa. Ahimsa is the soul of Truth. Man is mere animal without it. A seeker after Truth will realize all this in his search for Truth and he will then have no difficulty in the interpretation of the shastras.

Another canon of interpretation is to scan not the letter but to examine the spirit. Tulsidas's Ramayana is a notable book because it is informed with the spirit of purity, pity and piety. There is a verse in it which brackets drums, shudras, fools and women together as fit to be beaten. A man who cites that verse to beat his wife is doomed to perdition. Rama did not only not beat his wife, but never even sought to displease her. Tulsidas simply inserted in his poem a proverb current in his days, little dreaming that there would be brutes justifying beating of their wives on the authority of the verse.

But assuming that Tulsidas himself followed a custom which was prevalent in his days and beat his wife, what then? The beating was still wrong. But the Ramayana was not written to justify beating of wives by their husbands. It was written to depict Rama, the perfect man, and Sita the ideal wife, and Bharata the ideal of a devoted brother. Any justification incidentally met with therein of vicious customs should therefore be rejected.

Tulsidas did not write his priceless epic to teach geography, and any wrong geography that we happen to come across in Ramayana should be summarily rejected.

Let us examine the Gita in the light of these observations. Self-realization and its means is the theme of the Gita, the fight between two armies being but the occasion to expound the theme. You might, if you like, say that the Poet himself was not against war or violence and hence he did not hesitate to press the occasion of a war into service. But a reading of the Mahabharata has given me an altogether different impression. The poet Vyasa has demonstrated the futility of war by means of that epic of wonderful beauty.

What, he asks, if the Kauravas were vanquished? And what if the Pandavas won? How many were left of the victors and what was their lot? What an end Mother Kunti came to? And where are the Yadawas today? Where the description of the fight and justification of violence are not the subject-matter of the epic, it is quite wrong to emphasize those aspects. And if it is difficult to reconcile certain verses with the teaching of non-violence, it is far more difficult to set the whole of the Gita in the framework of violence.

The poet when he writes is not conscious of all the interpretations his composition is capable of. The beauty of poetry is that the creation transcends the poet. The Truth that he reaches in the highest flights of his fancy is often not to be met with in his life. The life story of many a poet thus belies his poetry. That the central teaching of the Gita is not himsa but ahimsa is amply demonstrated by the subject begun in the second chapter and summarized in the concluding 18th chapter.

The treatment in the other chapters also supports the position. Himsa is impossible without anger, without attachment, without hatred, and the Gita strives to carry us to the state beyond sattwa, rajas and tamas, a state that excludes anger, hatred etc. But I can even now picture to my mind Arjuna's eyes red with anger every time he drew the bow to the end of his ear.

It was not in a spirit of ahimsa that Arjuna refused to go to battle. He had fought many a battle before. Only this time he was overcome with false pity. He fought shy of killing his own kith and kin. Arjuna never discussed the problem of killing his kith and kin. Arjuna never discussed the problem of killing as such. He did not say he would kill no one, even if he regarded him as wicked.

Shri Krishna knows every one's innermost thoughts and he saw through the temporary infatuation of Arjuna. He therefore told him: 'Thou hast already done the killing. Thou canst not all at once argue thyself into non-violence. Finish what thou hast already begun.' If a passenger going in a Scotch Express gets suddenly sick of travelling and jumps out of it, he is guilty of suicide. He has not learnt the futility of travelling or travelling by a railway train. Similar was the case with Arjuna. Non-violent Krishna could give Arjuna no other advice. But to say that the Gita teaches violence or justifies war, because advice to kill was given a particular occasion, is as wrong as to say that himsa is the law of life, because a certain amount of it is inevitable in daily life.

To one who reads the spirit of the Gita, it teaches the secret of non-violence, the secret of realizing the self through the physical body. And who are Dhritarashtra and Yudhishthira and Arjuna? Who is Krishna? Were they all historical characters? And does the Gita describe them as such? Is it true that Arjuna suddenly stops in the midst of the fight and puts the question to Krishna, and Krishna repeats the whole of the Gita before him? And which is that Gita—the Gita that Arjuna forgot after having exclaimed that his infatuation was gone and which he requested Krishna to sing again, but which he could not, and which therefore he gave in the form of Anugita? I regard Duryodhana and his party as the baser impulses in man, and Arjuna and his party as the higher impulses. The field of battle is our own body. An eternal battle is going on between the two camps and the Poet Seer has vividly described it. Krishna is the Dweller within, ever whispering in a pure heart. Like the watch the heart needs the winding of purity, or the Dweller ceases to speak.

Not that actual physical battle is out of the question. To those who are innocent of non-violence, the Gita does not teach a lesson of despair. He who fears, who saves his skin, who yields to his passions, must fight the physical battle whether he will or no; but that is not his dharma. Dharma is one and one only. Ahimsa means moksha, and moksha is the realization of Truth. There is no room here for cowardice. Himsa will go on eternally in this strange world. The Gita shows the way out of it. But it also shows that escape out of cowardice and despair is not the way. Better far than cowardice is killing and being killed in battle.

If the meaning of the verses quoted by the correspondent is not still clear, I must confess my inability to make it so. Is it agreed that that the Almighty God is the Creator, Protector and Destroyer and ought to be such? And if He creates, He has undoubtedly the right to destroy. And yet He does not destroy because He does not create. His law is that whatever is born must die, and in that lies His mercy. His laws are immutable. Where should we all be if He changed them capriciously?

—Gandhi, M.K., *Young India*,
12 November 1925.

28

The Gita in My Understanding

Even in 1888–89, when I first became acquainted with the Gita, I felt that it was not a historical work, but that under the guise of physical warfare, it described the duel that perpetually went on in the hearts of mankind, and that physical warfare was brought in merely to make the description of the internal duel more alluring. This preliminary intuition became more confirmed on a closer study of religion and the Gita. A study of the Mahabharata gave it added confirmation. I do not regard the Mahabharata as a historical work in the accepted sense. The Adiparva contains powerful evidence in support of my opinion. By ascribing to the chief actors superhuman or subhuman origins, the great Vyasa made short work of the history of kings and their peoples. The persons therein described may be historical, but the author of the Mahabharata has used them merely to drive home his religious theme.

The author of the Mahabharata has not established the necessity of physical warfare; on the contrary he has proved its futility. He has made the victors shed tears of sorrow and repentance, and has left them nothing but a legacy of miseries. In this great work the Gita is the crown. Its second chapter, instead of teaching the rules of physical warfare, tells us how a perfected man is to be known. In the characteristics of the perfected man of the Gita, I do not see any to correspond to physical warfare. Its whole design is inconsistent with the rules of conduct governing the relations between warring parties.

Krishna of the Gita is perfection and right knowledge personified; but the picture is imaginary. That does not mean that Krishna, the adored of his people, never lived. But perfection is imagined. The idea of a perfect incarnation is an after growth.

In Hinduism, incarnation is ascribed to one who has performed some extraordinary service of mankind. All embodied life is in reality an incarnation of God, but it is not usual to consider every living being an incarnation. Future generations pay this homage to one who, in his own generation, has been extraordinarily religious in his conduct. I can see nothing wrong in this procedure; it takes nothing from God's greatness, and there is no violence done to Truth. There is an Urdu saying which means, 'Adam is not God but he is a spark of the Divine.' And therefore he who is the most religiously behaved has most of the divine spark in him. It is in accordance with this train of thought that Krishna enjoys, in Hinduism, the status of the most perfect incarnation.

This belief in incarnation is a testimony of man's lofty spiritual ambition. Man is not at peace with himself till he has become like unto God. The endeavour to reach this state is the supreme, the only ambition worth having. And this is self-realization. This self-realization is the subject of the Gita, as it is of all scriptures. But its author surely did not write it to establish that doctrine.

The Gita in My Understanding

The object of the Gita appears to me to be that of showing the most excellent way to attain self-realization. That which is to be found, more or less clearly, spread out here and there in Hindu religious books, has been brought out in the clearest possible language in the Gita even at the risk of repetition.

That matchless remedy is renunciation of the fruits of action. This is the centre round which the Gita is woven. This renunciation is the central sun, round which devotion, knowledge and the rest revolve like planets. The body has been likened to a prison. There must be action where there is body. Not one embodied being is exempted from labour. And yet all religions proclaim that it is possible for man, by treating the body as the temple of God, to attain freedom. Every action is tainted, be it ever so trivial. How can the body be made the temple of God? In other words how can one be free from action, i.e. from the taint of sin? 'By desireless action; by renouncing the fruits of action; by dedicating all activities to God, i.e. by surrendering oneself to Him body and soul.'

But desirelessness or renunciation does not come for the mere talking about it. It is not attained by an intellectual feat. It is attainable only by a constant heart-churn. Right knowledge is necessary for attaining renunciation. Learned men possess a knowledge of a kind. They may recite the Vedas from memory, yet they may be steeped in self- indulgence. In order that knowledge may not run riot, the author of the Gita has insisted on devotion accompanying it and has given it the first place. Knowledge without devotion will be like a misfire. Therefore, says the Gita, 'Have devotion, and knowledge will follow.' This devotion is not mere lip-worship, it is a wrestling with death. Hence the Gita's assessment of the devotee's qualities is similar to that of the sage's.

Thus the devotion required by the Gita is no softhearted effusiveness. It certainly is not blind faith. The devotion of the Gita has the least to do with externals. A devotee may use, if he likes, rosaries, forehead marks, make offerings, but these things are no test of his devotion. He is the devotee who is jealous of none, who is a fount of mercy, who is without egotism, who is selfless, who treats alike cold and heat, happiness and misery, who is ever forgiving, who is always contented, whose resolutions are firm, who has dedicated mind and soul to God, who causes no dread, who is not afraid of others, who is free from exultation, sorrow and fear, who is pure, who is versed in action and yet remains unaffected by it, who renounces all fruit, good or bad, who treats friend and foe alike, who is untouched by respect or disrespect, who is not puffed up by praise, who does not go under when people speak ill of him, who loves silence and solitude, who has a disciplined reason. Such devotion is inconsistent with the existence at the same time of strong attachments.

We thus see, that to be a real devotee is to realize oneself. Self-realization is not something apart. One rupee can purchase for us poison or nectar, but knowledge or devotion cannot buy us either salvation or bondage. These are not media of exchange. They are themselves the thing we want. In other words if the means and the end are not identical, they are almost so. The extreme of means is salvation. Salvation of the Gita is perfect peace.

But such knowledge and devotion, to be true, have

to stand the test of renunciation of fruits of action. Mere knowledge of right and wrong will not make one fit for salvation. According to common notions, a mere learned man will pass as a pandit. He need not perform any service. He will regard it as bondage even to lift a little lota. Where one test of knowledge is non-liability for service, there is no room for such mundane work as the lifting of a lota.

Or take bhakti. The popular notion of bhakti is soft-heartedness, telling beads and the like and disdaining to do even a loving service, lest the telling of beads etc. might be interrupted. This bhakta therefore leaves the rosary only for eating, drinking and the like, never for grinding corn or nursing patients.

But the Gita says: 'No one has attained his goal without action. Even men like Janaka attained salvation through action. If even I were lazily to cease working, the world would perish. How much more necessary then for the people at large to engage in action?'

While on the one hand it is beyond dispute that all action binds, on the other hand it is equally true that all living beings have to do some work whether they will or no. Here all activity, whether mental or physical, is to be included in the term action. Then how is one to be free from the bondage of action, even though he may be acting? The manner in which the Gita has solved the problem is, to my knowledge, unique. The Gita says: 'Do your allotted work but renounce its fruit—be detached and work—have no desire for reward and work.' This is the unmistakable teaching of the Gita. He who gives up action falls. He who gives up only the reward rises. But renunciation of fruit in no way means indifference to the result. In regard to every action one must know the result that is expected to follow, the means there to, and the capacity for it. He, who, being thus equipped, is without desire for the result, and is yet wholly engrossed in the due fulfilment of the task before him, is said to have renounced the fruits of his action.

Again, let no one consider renunciation to mean want of fruit for the renouncer. The Gita reading does not warrant such a meaning. Renunciation means absence of hankering after fruit. As a matter of fact, he who renounces reaps a thousandfold. The renunciation of the Gita is the acid test of faith. He who is ever brooding over result often loses nerve in the performance of his duty. He becomes impatient and then gives vent to anger and begins to do unworthy things; he jumps from action to action, never remaining faithful to any. He who broods over results is like a man given to objects of senses; he is ever distracted, he says goodbye to all scruples, everything is right in his estimation and he therefore resorts to means fair and foul to attain, his end.

From the bitter experiences of desire for fruit the author of the Gita discovered the path of renunciation of fruit, and put it before the world in most convincing manner. The common belief is that religion is always opposed to material good. 'One cannot act religiously in mercantile and such other matters. There is no place for religion in such pursuits; religion is only for attainment of salvation,' we hear many wordly-wise people say. In my opinion the author of the Gita has dispelled this delusion. He has drawn no line of demarcation between salvation and wordly pursuits. On the contrary, he has shown that religion must rule even our worldly pursuits. I have felt that the Gita teaches us that what cannot be followed out in day-to-day practice cannot be called religion. Thus, according to the Gita, all acts that are incapable of being performed without attachment are taboo. This golden rule saves mankind from many a pitfall. According to this interpretation murder, lying, dissoluteness and the like must be regarded as sinful and therefore taboo. Man's life then becomes simple, and from that simpleness springs peace.

Thinking along these lines, I have felt that in trying to enforce in one's life the central teaching of the Gita, one is bound to follow truth and ahimsa. When there is no desire for fruit, there is no temptation for untruth or himsa. Take any instance of untruth or violence, and it will be found that at its back was the desire to attain the cherished end. But it may be freely admitted that the Gita was not written to establish ahimsa. It was an accepted and primary duty even before the Gita age. The Gita had to deliver the message of renunciation of fruit. This is clearly brought out as early as the second chapter.

But if the Gita believed in ahimsa or it was included in desirelessness, why did the author take a warlike illustration? When the Gita was written, although people believed in ahimsa, wars were not only not taboo, but nobody observed the contradiction between them and ahimsa.

In assessing the implications of renunciation of fruit, we are not required to probe the mind of the author of the Gita as to his limitations of ahimsa and the like. Because a poet puts a particular truth before the world, it does not necessarily follow that he has known or worked out all its great consequences, or that having done so, he is able always to express them fully. In this perhaps lies the greatness of the poem and the poet. A poet's meaning is limitless. Like man, the meaning of great writings suffers evolution. On examining the history of languages, we notice that the meaning of important words has changed or expanded. This is true of the Gita. The author has himself extended the meanings of some of the current words. We are able to discover this even on a superficial examination. It is possible, that in the age prior to that of the Gita, offering of animals in sacrifice was permissible. But there is not a trace of it in the sacrifice in the Gita sense. In the Gita continuous concentration on God is the king of sacrifices. The third chapter seems to show that sacrifice chiefly means body-labour for service. The third and the fourth chapters read together will give us other meanings for sacrifice but never animal-sacrifice.

Similarly has the meaning of the word sannyasa undergone, in the Gita, a transformation. The sannyasa of the Gita will not tolerate complete cessation of all activity. The sannyasa of the Gita is all work and yet no work. Thus the author of the Gita by extending meanings of words has taught us to imitate him. Let it be granted, that according to the letter of the Gita it is possible to say that warfare is consistent with renunciation of fruit. But after 40 years' unremitting endeavour fully to enforce the teaching of the Gita in my own life, I have, in all humility, felt that perfect renunciation is impossible without perfect observance of ahimsa in every shape and form.

The Gita is not an aphoristic work; it is a great religious poem. The deeper you dive into it, the richer the meanings you get. It being meant for the people at large, there is pleasing repetition.

With every age the important words will carry new and expanding meanings. But its central teaching will never vary. The seeker is at liberty to extract from this treasure any meaning he likes so as to enable him to enforce in his life the central teaching.

Nor is the Gita a collection of Do's and Don'ts. What is lawful for one may be unlawful for another. What may be permissible at one time, or in one place, may not be so at another time, and in another place. Desire for fruit is the only universal prohibition. Desirelessness is obligatory.

The Gita has sung the praises of knowledge, but it is beyond the mere intellect; it is essentially addressed to the heart and capable of being understood by the heart. Therefore the Gita is not for those who have no faith. The author makes Krishna say:

> Do not entrust this treasure to him who is without sacrifice, without devotion, without the desire for this teaching and who denies Me. On the other hand those who will give this precious treasure to My devotees will by the fact of this service assuredly reach Me. And those who, being free from malice, will with faith absorb this teaching, shall, having attained freedom, live where people of true merit go after death.

—Gandhi, M.K., *Young India*, 6 August 1931.

29

The Gita from Yeravda

I run to my Mother Gita whenever I find myself in difficulties and up to now she has never failed to comfort me. It is possible that those, who are getting comfort from the Gita, may get greater help, and see something altogether new, if they come to know the way in which I understand it from day to day.

This day I feel like giving a summary of the twelfth chapter. It is Bhaktiyoga—realization of God through devotion. At the time of marriage we ask the bridal couple to learn this chapter by heart and meditate upon it, as one of the five sacrifices to be performed. Without devotion, action and knowledge are cold and dry, and may even become shackles. So, with the heart full of love, let us approach this meditation on the Gita.

Arjuna asks of the Lord: 'Which is the better of the two, the devotee who worships the Manifest or the one who worships the Unmanifest?'

The Lord says in reply: 'Those who meditate on the Manifest in full faith, and lose themselves in Me, those faithful ones are My devotees. But those who worship the Unmanifest, and who, in order to do so, restrain all their senses, look upon and serve all alike, regarding none as high or low, those also realize Me.'

So it cannot be affirmed that one is superior to the other. But it may be counted as impossible for an embodied being fully to comprehend and adore the Unmanifest. The Unmanifest is attributeless, and is beyond the reach of human vision. Therefore all embodied beings, consciously or unconsciously, are devotees of the Manifest.

'So,' saith the Lord, 'let thy mind be merged in My Universal Body, which has form. Offer thy all at His feet. But if thou canst not do this, practise the restraint of the passions of thy mind. By observing yama and niyama with the help of pranayama, asana and other practices, bring the mind under control. If thou canst not do thus, then perform all thy works with this in mind: that whatever work thou undertakest, that thou dost for My sake. Thus thy worldly infatuations and attachments will fade away, and gradually thou wilt become stainless and pure. The fountain of love will rise in thee. But if thou canst not do even this, then renounce the fruit of all thy actions; yearn no more after the fruits of thy work. Ever do that work which falls to thy lot. Man cannot be master over the fruits of his work. The fruit of work appears only after causes have combined to form it.

Therefore be thou only the instrument. Do not regard as superior or inferior any of these four methods which I have shown unto thee. Whatever, in them, is suitable for thee, that make thou use of in thy practice of devotion.

'It seems that the path of hearing, meditating and comprehending, may be easier than the path of yama, niyama, pranayama and asana, to which I have referred; easier than that may be concentration and worhip; and again easier than concentration may be renunciation of the fruits of works. The same method cannot be equally easy for every one; some may have to turn for help to all these methods. They are certainly intermixed.

In any case thou wishest to be a devotee. Achieve that goal by whatever method thou canst. My part is simply to tell thee whom to count a true devotee. A devotee hates no one; bears no grudge against any one; befriends all creatures; is merciful to all. To accomplish this he eliminates all personal attachments; his ego is dissolved and he becomes as nothing; for him grief and happiness are one; he forgives those who trespass against himself, as he hungers for forgiveness from the world for his own faults; he dwells in contentment; he is firm in his good resolves; he surrenders to Me his mind, his intellect, his all. He never causes in other beings trouble or fear, himself knowing no trouble or fear through others My devotee is free from joy and sorrow, pleasure and pain. He has no desires, he is pure, skilful and wise. He has renounced all ambitious undertakings. He stands by his resolves, renouncing their good or bad fruit; he remains unconcerned. Such a one knows not enemies or friends, is beyond honour or disgrace.

'In peace and silence, contented with whatever may come his way, he lives inwardly as if alone, and always remains calm no matter what may be going around him. One who lives in this manner, full of faith, he is My "beloved devotee".'

—Gandhi, M.K., *Young India*,
13 November 1930.

30

The Philosophy of Non-Violence

When a person claims to be non-violent, he is expected not to be angry with one who has injured him. He will not wish him harm; he will wish him well; he will not swear at him; he will not cause him any physical hurt. He will put up with all the injury to which he is subjected by the wrongdoer.

Thus non-violence is complete innocence. Complete non-violence is complete absence of ill-will against all that lives. It therefore embraces even sub-human life not excluding noxious insects or beasts. They have not been created to feed our destructive propensities. If we only knew the mind of the Creator, we should find their proper place in His creation.

Non-violence is therefore in its active form goodwill towards all life. It is pure love. I read it in the Hindu Scriptures, in the Bible, in the Quran. Non-violence is a perfect state. It is a goal towards which all mankind moves naturally though unconsciously. Man does not become divine when he personifies innocence in himself. Only then does he become truly man.

In our present state we are partly men and partly beasts and in our ignorance and even arrogance say that we truly fulfil the purpose of our species, when we deliver blow for blow and develop the measure of anger required for the purpose. We pretend to believe that retaliation is the law of our being, whereas in every scripture we find that retaliation is nowhere obligatory but only permissible.

It is restraint that is obligatory. Retaliation is indulgence requiring elaborate regulating. Restraint is the law of our being. For, highest perfection is unattainable without highest restraint. Suffering is thus the badge of the human tribe.

A true pacifist is a true satyagrahi. The latter acts by faith and, therefore, is not concerned about the result, for he knows that it is assured when the action is true. ...Pacifists have to prove their faith by resolutely refusing to do anything with war, whether of defense or offence.

—Gandhi, M.K., *Young India*,
3 March 1922.

31

On Change of Faith

C.F. Andrews: 'What would you say to a man who after considerable thought and prayer said that he could not have his peace and salvation except by becoming a Christian?'

Gandhiji: 'I would say if a non-Christian (say a Hindu) came to a Christian and made that statement, he should ask him to become a good Hindu rather than find goodness in change of faith.'

C.F.A.: 'I cannot in this go the whole length with you, though you know my own position. I discarded the position that there is no salvation except through Christ long ago. But supposing the Oxford Group Movement people changed the life of your son, and he felt like being converted, what would you say?'

Gandhiji: 'I would say that the Oxford Group may change the lives of as many as they like, but not their religion. They can draw their attention to the best in their respective religions and change their lives by asking them to live according to them. There came to me a man, the son of brahmana parents, who said his reading of your book had led him to embrace Christianity. I asked him if he thought that the religion of his forefathers was wrong. He said, "No."

Then I said: "Is there any difficulty about your accepting the Bible as one of the great religious books of the world and Christ as one of the great teachers?" I said to him that you had never through your books asked Indians to take up the Bible and embrace Christianity, and that he had misread your book—unless of course your position is like that of the late M. Mahomed Ali's, viz. that "a believing Mussulman, however bad his life, is better than a good Hindu".'

C.F.A.: 'I do not accept M. Mahomed Ali's position at all. But, I do say that if a person really needs a change of faith I should not stand in his way.'

Gandhiji: 'But don't you see that you do not even give him a chance? You do not even cross-examine him. Supposing a Christian came to me and said he was captivated by a reading of the Bhagawata and so wanted to declare himself a Hindu, I should say him: "No. What the Bhagawata offers the Bible also offers. You have not yet made the attempt to find it out. Make the attempt and be a good Christian".'

C.F.A.: 'I don't know. If someone earnestly says that he will become a good Christian, I should say, "You may become one", though you know that I have in my own life strongly dissuaded ardent enthusiasts who came to me. I said to them, "Certainly not on my account will you do anything of the kind." But human nature does require a concrete faith.'

Gandhiji: 'If a person wants to believe in the Bible let him say so, but why should he discard his own religion? This proselytization will mean no peace in the world. Religion is a very personal matter. We should by living the life according to our lights share the best with one another, thus adding to the sum total of human effort to reach God.'

'Consider,' continued Gandhiji, 'whether you are going to accept the position of mutual toleration or of equality of all religions. My position is that all the great religions are fundamentally equal. We must have innate respect for other religions as we have for our own. Mind you, not mutual toleration, but equal respect.'

—Gandhi, M.K., *Harijan*, 28 November 1936.

I have had the privilege of having under me Mussulman, Parsi and Christian minors. Never was Hinduism put before them for their acceptance. They were encouraged and induced to respect and read their own scriptures. It is with pleasure that I can recall instances of men and women, boys and girls having been induced to know and love their faiths better than they did before if they were also encouraged to study the other faiths with sympathy and respect. We have in the Ashram today several faiths represented. No proselytizing is practised or permitted. We recognize that all these faiths are true and divinely inspired, and all have suffered through the necessarily imperfect handling of imperfect men.

My fear is that though Christian friends nowadays do not say or admit that Hindu religion is untrue, they must harbour in the breasts the belief that Hinduism is an error and that Christianity as they believe it is the only true religion. Without some such thing it is not possible to understand, much less to appreciate, the C.M.S. appeal from which I reproduced in these columns some revealing extracts the other day.

One could understand the attack on untouchability and many other errors that have crept into Hindu life. And if they would help us to get rid of the admitted abuses and purify our religion, they would do helpful constructive work which would be gratefully accepted. But so far as one can understand the present effort, it is to uproot Hinduism from the very foundation and replace it by another faith.

It is like an attempt to destroy a house which though badly in want of repair appears to the dweller quite decent and habitable. No wonder he welcomes those who show him how to repair it and even offer to do so themselves. But he would most decidedly resist those who sought to destroy that house that had served well with him and his ancestors for ages, unless he, the dweller, was convinced that the house was beyond repair and unfit for human habitation.

If the Christian world entertains that opinion about the Hindu house, 'Parliament of Religions' and 'International Fellowship' are empty phrases. For both the terms presuppose equality of status, a common platform. There cannot be a common platform as between inferiors and superiors, or the enlightened and unenlightened, the regenerate and the unregenerate, the high-born and the low-born, the caste-man and the outcaste. My comparison may be defective, may even sound offensive.

My reasoning may be unsound. But my proposition stands.

—Gandhi, M.K., *Harijan*, 26 December 1936.

32

The Way to Peace

I do suggest that the doctrine [of non-violence] holds good also as between States and States. I know that I am treading on delicate ground if I refer to the late War. But I fear I must, in order to make the position clear. It was a war of aggrandizement, as if have understood, on either part. It was a war for dividing the spoils of the exploitation of weaker races-otherwise euphemistically called the world commence... It would be found that, before general disarmament in Europe commences, as it must some day unless Europe is to commit suicide, some nation will have to dare to disarm herself and take large risks. The level of non-violence in that nation, if that every happily comes to pass, will naturally have risen so high as to command universal respect. Her judgments will be unerring, her decision firm, her capacity for heroic self-sacrifice will be great, and she will want to live as much for other nations as for herself.

—Gandhi, M.K., *Young India,* 8 October 1925, p. 345.

Like opium production, the world manufacture of swords needs to be restricted. The sword is probably responsible for more misery in the world than opium...

'Since disarmament chiefly depends on Great Power

why should Switzerland, which is a small State and a neutral State, be asked to disarm itself?' It is from the neutral ground of your country that I am speaking to all other powers and not only to Switzerland. If you won't carry this message to other parts of Europe, I shall be absolved from all blame. And seeing that Switzerland is a neutral territory and non-aggressive nation, there is all the more reason why Switzerland should not need an army. Secondly, it is through your hospitality and by reason of your occupying the vantage ground that you have nationals coming to you. It should be possible for you to give to the world a lesson tin disarmament and show that you are brave enough to do without an army.

—Gandhi, M.K., *Young India*,
19 November 1925, p. 397.

'How could a disarmed neutral country allow other nations to be destroyed? But for our army which was waiting ready at our frontier during the last war we should have been ruined.'

At the risk of being considered a visionary or a fool I must answer this question in the only manner I know. It would be cowardly of a neutral country to allow an army to devastate a neighbouring country. But there are two ways in common between soldiers of war and soldier of non-violence, and if I had been a citizen of Switzerland and President of the Federal State, what I would have done would be to refuse passage to the invading army by refusing all supplies. Secondly, by reenacting a Thermopylx in Switzerland, you would have presented a living wall of men and woman and children, inviting invaders to walk over your corpses. You may say that such a thing is beyond human experience and endurance. I say that it is not so. It was quite possible. Last year in Gujarat, women stood *lathi* charges unflinchingly, and in Peshawar, thousands stood hails of bullets without resorting to violence. Imagine these men and women staying in front of an army requiring a safe passage to another country. The army would be brutal enough to walk over them, you might say. I would then say you will still have done your duty by allowing yourself to be annihilated. An army that dares to pass over the corpses of innocent men and women would not be able to repeat that experiment. You may, if you wish, refuse to believe in such courage on the part of the masses of men and women, but, then, you would have to admit that non-violence is made of sterner stuff. It was never conceived as a weapon of the weak but of the stoutest hearts.

—Gandhi, M.K., *Young India*,
31 December 1931, p. 427.

It is... open to the Great Powers to take it [non-violence] up any day and cover themselves with glory and earn the eternal gratitude of posterity. If they or any of them could shed the fear of destruction, if they disarmed themselves, they will automatically help the rest to regain their sanity. But, then, these Great Power have to give up imperialistic ambitions and exploitation of the so-called uncivilized or semi-civilized nations of the earth and revise their mode of life. It means a complete revolution. Great nations can hardly be expected, in the ordinary course, to move spontaneously in a direction the reverse of the one they have followed, and according to their notion of values, from victory to victory. But miracles have happened before and may happen even in this very prosaic age. Who can dare limit God's power of undoing wrong? One thing is certain. If the mad race for armaments continues, it is bound to result in a slaughter such as has never occurred in history. If there is a victor left, the very victory will be a living death for the nation that emerges victorious. There is no escape from the impending doom save through a bold and unconditional acceptance of the non-violent method with all its glorious implications.

—Gandhi, M.K., *Harijan*, 28 November 1938.

'What to do with 'gangster' nations, if I may the expression frequently used? There was individual gangsterism in America. It has been put down by strong police measures both local and national. Could not we do something similar for gangsterism between nations, as instanced in Manchuria-the nefarious use of the opium poison, in Abyssinia, in Spain, in the sudden seizure of Austria, and then, the case of Czechoslovakia?' if the best minds of the world have not imbibed the spirit of non-violence, they would have to meet gansterism in the orthodox way. But that would only show that we have not got far beyond the law of the jungle, that we have not yet learnt to appreciate the heritage that God has given us, that, in spite of the teaching of Christianity which is 1900 years old and of Hinduism and Buddhism which are older, and even of Islam (if I have read it aright), we have not made much headway as human beings. But, whilst I would understand the use of force by those who have not the spirit of non-violence to throw their whole weight in demonstrating that even gangsterism has to be met by non-violence. For, ultimately, force, however justifiably used, will lead us into the same morass as the force of Hitler and Mussolini. There will be just a difference of degree. You and I who believe in non-violence must use it at the critical moment. We may not despair of touching the hearts even of gangsters, even if, for the moment, we may seem to be striking our heads against a blind wall.

—Gandhi, M.K., *Harijan*, 10 December 1938, p. 372.

When the position is examined in terms of non-violence, I must say it is unbecoming of a great nation of 400 millions, a nation as cultured as China, to repel Japanese aggression by resorting to Japan's own methods. If the Chinese had non-violence of my conception, there would be no use left for the latest machinery for destruction which Japan possesses. The Chinese would say to Japan, 'Bring all your machinery, we present half of our population to you. But, the remaining 200 millions won't bend their knee to you'. If the Chinese did that, Japan would become China's slave.

—Gandhi, M.K., *Harijan*, 24 December 1936, p. 394.

[F]or the Poles to stand valiantly against the German hordes, vastly superior in numbers, military equipment and strength, was almost non-violence. I should not mind repeating that statement over and over again. You must give its full value to the word 'almost'. But we are 400 millions here. If we were to organize a big army and prepare ourselves to fight foreign aggression, how could we by any stretch of imagination call ourselves almost non-violent, let alone non-violent? The Poles were unprepared for the way in which the enemy swooped down upon them. When we talk of armed preparation, we contemplate preparation to meet any violent combination with our superior violence. If India ever prepared herself that way, she would constitute the greatest menace to world peace. For, if we take that path, we will also have to choose the path of exploitation like the European nations.

—Gandhi, M.K., *Harijan*, 25 August 1940, p. 261.

It may be long before the law of love will be recognized in international affairs. The machineries of Governments stand between and hide the hearts of one people from those of another. Yet... we can see how the world is moving steadily to realize that between nation and nation, as between man and man, force has failed to solve problems, but that the economic sanction of non-co-operation is far more mighty and conclusive than armies and navies.

Till a new energy is harnessed and put on wheels, the captains of older energies will treat the innovation as theoretical, impractical, idealistic and so on. It may take long to lay the wires for international love, but the sanction of international non-co-operation in preference to continued physical compulsion [...] is a distinct progress towards the ultimate and real solution.

—Gandhi, M.K., *Harijan*, 28 November 1936, p. 51.

Not to believe in the possibility of permanent peace is to disbelieve in the Godliness of human nature. Methods hereto adopted have failed because rock-bottom sincerity on the part of those who have striven has been lacking. Not that they have realized this lack. Peace is unattained by part performance of conditions, even as a chemical combination is impossible without complete fulfillment of the conditions of attainment thereof. If the recognized leaders of mankind who have control over the engines of destruction were wholly to renounce their use, with full knowledge of its implications, permanent peace can be obtained. This is clearly impossible without the Great Powers of the earth renouncing their imperialistic design. This, again, seems impossible without great nations ceasing to believe in soul-destroying competition and to desire to multiply wants and, therefore, increase their material possessions. It is my conviction that the root of the evil is want of a living faith in a living God. It is a first-class human tragedy that peoples of the earth who claim to believe tin the message of Jesus, whom they describe as the Prince of Peace, show little of that belief in actual practice. It is painful to see sincere Christian divines limiting the scope of Jesus' message to select individuals. I have been taught from my childhood and tested the truth by experience that the primary virtues of mankind are possible of cultivation by the meanest of the human species. It is this undoubted universal possibility that distinguishes the humans from the rest of God's creation. If even one nation were unconditionally to perform the supreme act of renunciation, many of us would see in our life-time visible peace established on earth.

—Gandhi, M.K., *Harijan*, 18 June 1938, pp. 153–54.

Faith
. . . .

33

The Analogy of Faith

The closest, though very incomplete, analogy for religion I can find is marriage. It is or used to be an indissoluble tie. Much more so is the tie of religion.

Just as a husband does not remain faithful to his wife, or wife to her husband, because either is conscious of some exclusive superiority of the other over the rest of his or her sex but because of some indefinable but irresistible attraction, so does one remain irresistibly faithful to one's own religion and find full satisfaction in such adhesion.

And just as a faithful husband does not need in order to sustain his faithfulness, to consider other women as inferior to his wife, so does not a person belonging to one religion need to consider others to be inferior to his own. To pursue the analogy still further, even as faithfulness to one's wife does not presuppose blindness to her shortcomings, so does not faithfulness to one's religion presuppose blindness to the shortcomings of that religion.

Indeed, faithfulness, not blind adherence, demands a keener perception of shortcomings and therefore a livelier sense of the proper remedy for their removal. Taking the view I do of religion, it is unnecessary for me to examine the beauties of Hinduism. The reader may rest assured that I am not likely to remain Hindu if I was not conscious of its many beauties. Only for my purpose they need not be exclusive. My approach to other religions, therefore, is never as a fault-finding critic but as a devotee hoping to find the like beauties in other religions and wishing to incorporate in my own the good I may find in them and miss in mine.

—Gandhi, M.K., *Harijan*, 12 August 1933, p. 4.

In spite of my being a staunch Hindu I find room in my faith for Christian and Islamic and Zoroastrian teaching, and, therefore, my Hinduism *seems* to some to be a conglomeration and some have even dubbed me an eclectic.

—Gandhi, M.K., *Young India*, 22 December 1927, p. 425.

Well, to call a man eclectic is to say that he has no faith, but mine is a broad faith which does not oppose Christians— not even a Plymouth Brother—not even the most fanatical Mussalman. It is a faith based on the broadest possible toleration. I refuse to abuse a man for his fanatical deeds, because I try to see them from his point of view. It is that broad faith that sustains me. It is a somewhat embarrassing position I know—but to others, not to me.

—Gandhi, M.K., *Harijan*, 12 August 1933, p. 4.

34

My Faith in God

There are subjects where reason cannot take us far and we have to accept things on faith. Faith, then, does not contradict reason but transcends it. It is a kind of sixth sense which works in cases which are without the purview of reason.

—Gandhi, M.K., *Harijan*, 6 March 1937, p. 4.

It is faith that steers us through stormy seas, faith that moves mountains and faith that jumps across the ocean. That faith is nothing but a living, wide-awake consciousness of God within. He who has achieved that wants nothing. Bodily diseased, he is spiritually healthy; physically poor, he rolls in spiritual riches.

—Gandhi, M.K., *Young India*, 25 September 1925.

It only begins where reason stops. But there are very few actions in the world for which reasonable justification cannot be found. Experience has humbled me enough to let me realize the specific limitations of reason. Just as matter misplaced becomes dirt, reason misused becomes lunacy. Without faith this world would come to naught in a moment. True faith is appropriation of the reasoned experience of people whom we believe to have lived a life purified by prayer and penance. Belief, therefore, in prophets or incarnations who have lived in remote ages is not an idle superstition but a satisfaction of an inmost spiritual want.

—Gandhi, M.K., *Young India*, 24 June 1926.

I would have you brush aside all rational explanations and begin with a simple childlike faith in God. If I exist God exists. With me it is a necessity of my being as it is with millions. They may not be able to talk about it but from their lives you can see that it is a part of their life. I am only asking you to restore the belief that has been undermined. In order to do so you have to unlearn a lot of literature that dazzles your intelligence and throws you off your feet. Start with the faith which is also a token of humility and an admission that we know nothing, that we are less than atoms in this universe. We are less than atoms, I say, because the atom obeys the law of its being, whereas, we, in the insolence of our ignorance deny the law of nature. But I have no argument to address to those who have no faith.

—Gandhi, M.K., *Young India*, 24 September 1931, p. 274.

I claim to be a man of faith and prayer and even if I were to be cut to pieces, I trust God would give me the strength not to deny Him, but to assert that He is... I am surer of His existence than of the fact that you and I are sitting in this room. Then I can also testify that I may live without air and water but not without Him. You may pluck out my eyes, but that cannot kill me. You may chop off my nose, but that will not kill me. But blast my faith in God, and I am dead. You may call this a superstition, but I confess it is a superstition that I hug, even as I used to hug the name of Rama in my childhood when there was any cause of danger or alarm.

> —Gandhi, M.K., *From Yeravda Mandir: Ashram Observances*, Valji Govindji Desai (trans.), Navajivan Publishing House, 1933.

Everyone has faith in God though everyone does not know it. For, everyone has faith in himself and that multiplied to the nth degree is God. The sum total of all that lives is God. We may not be God but we are of God—even as a little drop of water is of the ocean. Imagine it torn away from the ocean and flung millions of miles away. It becomes helpless torn from its surroundings and cannot feel the might and majesty of the ocean. But if some one could point out to it that it is of the ocean, its faith would revive, it would dance with joy and the whole of the might and majesty of the ocean would be reflected in it.

> —Gandhi, M.K., *Harijan*, 3 September 1939.

Without faith this world would come to naught in a moment. True faith is appropriation of the reasoned experience of people whom we believe to have lived a life purified by prayer and penance. Belief, therefore, in prophets or incarnations who have lived in remote ages is not an idle superstition but a satisfaction of an inmost spiritual want.

> —Gandhi, M.K., *Young India*, 14 April 1927.

Seeing God face to face is to feel that He is enthroned in our hearts even as a child feels a mother's affection without needing any demonstration. Does a child reason out the existence of a mother's love? Can he prove it to others? He triumphantly declares, 'It is.' So must it be with the existence of God. He defies reason. But He is experienced. Let us not reject the experience of Tulasidas, Chaitanya, Ramadas and a host of other spiritual teachers even as we do not reject that of mundane teachers.

—Gandhi, M.K., *Harijan*, 3 June 1939.

35

My Belief in an Indefinable Power

There is an indefinable mysterious Power that pervades everything. I feel it, though I do not see it. It is this unseen Power which makes itself felt and yet defies all proof, because it is so unlike all that I perceive through my senses. It transcends the senses.

But it is impossible to reason out the existence of God to a limited extent. Even in ordinary affairs we know that people do not know who rules or why, and how he rules. And yet they know that there is a power that certainly rules.

In my tour last year in Mysore I met many poor villagers and I found upon inquiry that they did not know who ruled Mysore. They simply said some god ruled it. If the knowledge of these poor people was so limited about their ruler, I who am infinitely lesser than God, than they than their ruler, need not be surprised if I do not realize the presence of God the King of kings.

Nevertheless I do feel as the poor villagers felt about Mysore that there is orderliness in the Universe, there is an unalterable Law governing everything and every being that exists or lives. It is not a blind law; for no blind law can govern the conduct of living beings, and thanks to the marvellous researches of Sir J. C. Bose, it can now be proved that even matter is life.

That Law then which governs all life is God. Law and the Lawgiver are one. I may not deny the Law or the Law-giver, because I know so little about It or Him. Even as my denial or ignorance of the existence of an earthly power will avail me nothing, so will not my denial of God and His Law liberate me from its operation; whereas humble and mute acceptance of divine authority makes life's journey easier even as the acceptance of earthly rule makes life under it easier.

I do dimly perceive that whilst everything around me is ever changing, ever dying, there is underlying all that change a living power that is changeless, that holds all together, that creates, dissolves and recreates. That informing power or spirit is God. And since nothing else I see merely through the senses can or will persist, He alone is.

And is this power benevolent or malevolent? I see it is purely benevolent. For I can see that in the midst of death life persists, in the midst of untruth truth persists, in the midst of darkness light persists. Hence I gather that God is Life, Truth, Light. He is Love. He is the Supreme Good.

But He is no God who merely satisfies the intellect, if He ever does. God to be God must rule the heart and transform it. He must express Himself in every smallest act of His votary. This can only be done through a definite realization more real than the five senses can ever produce. Sense perceptions can be, often are, false and deceptive, however real they may appear to us. Where there is realization outside the senses it is infallible. It is proved not by extraneous evidence but in the transformed conduct and character of those who have felt the real presence of God within. Such testimony is to be found in the experiences of an unbroken line of prophets and sages in all countries and climes; To reject this evidence is to deny myself.

This realization is preceded by an immovable faith. He who would in his own person test the fact of 'God's presence can do so by a living faith. And since faith itself cannot be proved by extraneous evidence, the safest course is to believe in the moral government of the world and therefore in the supremacy of the moral law, the law of truth and love. Exercise of faith will be the safest where there is a clear determination summarily to reject all that is contrary to Truth and Love.

I cannot account for the existence of evil by any rational method. To want to do so is to be coequal with God. I am therefore humble enough to recognize evil as such. And I call God long suffering and patient precisely because He permits evil in the world. I know that He has no evil. He is the author of it and yet untouched by it.

I know too that I shall never know God if I do not wrestle with and against evil even at the cost of life itself. I am fortified in the belief by my own humble and limited experience. The purer I try to become, the nearer I feel to be to God. How much more should I be, when my faith is not a mere apology as it is today but has become as immovable as the Himalayas and as white and bright as the snows on their peaks? Meanwhile I invite the correspondent to pray with Newman who sang from experience:

> Lead, kindly Light, amid the encircling gloom,
> Lead Thou me on:
> The night is dark and I am far from home,

Lead Thou me on.
Keep Thou my feet, I do not ask to see
The distant scene; one step enough for me.

—Gandhi, M.K., *Young India*,
11 October 1928, p. 340.

36

The Voice of God

For me the Voice of God, of Conscience, of Truth or the Inner Voice or 'the still small Voice' mean one and the same thing. I saw no form. I have never tried, for I have always believed God to be without form. But what I did hear was like a Voice from afar and yet quite near. . It was as unmistakable as some human voice definitely speaking to me, and irresistible. I was not dreaming at the time I heard the Voice. The hearing of the Voice was preceded by a terrific struggle within me. Suddenly the Voice came upon me. I listened, made certain that it was the Voice, and the struggle ceased. I was calm. The determination was made accordingly, the date and the hour of the fast were fixed. Joy came over me. This was between 11 and 12 midnight. I felt refreshed and began to write the note about it which the reader must have seen.

Could I give any further evidence that it was truly the Voice that I heard and that it was not an echo of my own heated imagination? I have no further evidence to convince the sceptic. He is free to say that it was all self-delusion or hallucination. It may well have been so. I can offer no proof to the contrary. But I can say this that not the unanimous verdict of the whole world against me could shake me from the belief that what I heard was the true Voice of God.

But some think that God Himself is a creation of our own imagination. If that view holds good, then nothing is real, everything is of our own imagination. Even so, whilst my imagination dominates me, I can only act under its spell. Realest things are only relatively so. For me the Voice was more real than my own existence. It has never failed me, and for that matter, anyone else.

And every one who wills can hear the Voice. It is within every one. But like everything else, it requires previous and definite preparation.

—Gandhi, M.K., *Harijan*, 7 July 1933, p. 4.

This belief in God has to be based on faith which transcends reason. Indeed, even the so-called realization has at bottom an element of faith without which it cannot be sustained. In the very nature of things it must be so. Who can transgress the limitations of his being? I hold that complete realization is impossible in this embodied life. Nor is it necessary. A living immovable faith is all that is required for reaching the full spiritual height attainable by human beings. God is not outside this earthly case of ours. Therefore exterior proof is not of much avail, if any at all. We must ever fail to perceive Him through the senses, because He is beyond them. We can feel Him, if we will but withdraw ourselves from the senses. The divine music is incessantly going on within ourselves, but the loud senses drown the delicate music, which is unlike and infinitely superior to anything we can perceive or hear with our senses.

—Gandhi, M.K., *Harijan*, 13 June 1936, p. 140.

The Voice of God ▪ 153

It is easy enough to say, 'I do not believe in God. For God permits all things to be said of Him with impunity. He looks at our acts. And any breach of His law carries with it, not its vindictive, but its purifying, compelling, punishment. God's existence cannot be, does not need to be, proved. God is. If He is not felt, so much the worse for us. The absence of feeling is a disease which we shall some day throw off *nolens volens*.

—Gandhi, M.K., *Young India*,
23 September 1926, p. 33.

37

Many Yet One: My Experience with God

All faiths are a gift of God, but partake of human imperfection, as they pass through the medium of humanity. God-given religion is beyond all speech. Imperfect men put it into such language as they can command, and their words are interpreted by other men equally imperfect. Whose interpretation must be held to be the right one ? Every one is right from his own standpoint, but it is not impossible that every one is wrong. Hence the necessity for tolerance, which does not mean indifference towards one's own faith, but a more intelligent and purer love for it. Tolerance gives us spiritual insight, which is as far from fanaticism as the north pole is from the south. True knowledge of religion breaks down the barriers between faith and faith and gives rise to tolerance. Cultivation of tolerance for other faiths will impart to us a truer understanding of our own.

—Gandhi, M.K., *Young India*, 2 October 1930, p. 2.

God is an Idea, Law Himself... He and His Law abide everywhere and govern everything. Therefore, though I do not think that He answers in every detail, every request of ours, there is no doubt that He rules our actions and I literally believe that not a blade of grass grows or moves without His will.

—Gandhi, M.K., *Harijan*, 23 February 1940, p. 55.

I do feel that there is orderliness in the universe, there is an unalterable Law governing everything and every being that lives and moves. It is not a blind law, for no blind law can govern the conduct of living beings... The Law and the Law-giver are one. I may not deny the Law or Law-giver, because I know so little about It or Him. Even as my denial or ignorance of the existence of an earthly power will avail nothing, so will not my denial of God and His Law, liberate me from its operation; whereas, humble and mute acceptance of Divine Authority makes life's journey easier even as acceptance of earthly rule makes life under it easier...

—Gandhi, M.K.,' *My Spiritual Message*', 17 October 1931, Kingsley Hall, London, Address.

God is, even though the whole world deny Him. God embraces not only this tiny globe of ours, but millions and billions of such globes. How can we, little crawling creatures so utterly helpless as He has made us, how could we possibly measure His greatness, His boundless love, His infinite compassion? So great is His infinite love and pity that He allows man insolently to deny Him, wrangle about Him, and cut the throats of his fellowmen. How can we measure the greatness of God, who is so forgiving, so divine?

He allows us freedom and yet His compassion commands obedience to His Will. But if anyone of us disdains to bow to His Will, He says: 'So be it.' 'My sun will shine no less for thee, My clouds will rain no less for thee. I need not force thee to accept My sway.' Of such a God let the ignorant dispute the existence. I am one of the millions of wise men who believe in Him and am never tired of bowing to Him and singing His glory.

—Gandhi, M.K., *Young India*,
21 January 1926, pp. 30–31.

God is the hardest task-master, I have known on earth. He tries you through and through. And when you find your faith is failing, or your body is failing you, and you are sinking, He comes to your assistance somehow or other and proves to you that you must not lose your faith and that He is always at your beck and call, but on His terms. So I have found. I cannot recall a single instance when at the eleventh hour, He has forsaken me. There is only one omnipotent and omnipresent God. He is named variously and we remember Him by the name which is most familiar to us. Each person can choose the name that appeals most to him. Ishwara, Allah, Khuda, God mean the same.

God has a thousand names, or rather, He is nameless. We may worship or pray to Him by whichever name that pleases us. All worship the same Spirit, but as all foods do not agree with all, all names do not appeal to all. Each chooses the name according to His associations and He being the Indweller All-Powerful and Omniscient, knows our inmost feelings and responds to us according to our deserts.

In my opinion, Rama, Rahaman, Ahurmazda, God or Krishna, are all attempts on the part of man to name that invisible Force...Man can only conceive God within the limitations of his own mind. What matters, then, whether one man worships God as a person and another as Force? Both do right according to their lights. One need only remember that God is the Force among all the forces. All other forces are material. But God is the Vital Force or Spirit which is all-pervading, all-embracing and therefore beyond human ken.

Daridranarayan is one of millions of names by which humanity knows God who is unnameable and unfathomable by human understanding. And it means God of the poor, God appearing in the hearts of the poor.

God is not a person. To affirm that He descends to earth every now and again, in the form of human being, is a partial truth, which merely signifies that such a person lives near to God. Inasmuch as God is omnipresent, He dwells within every human being and all may, therefore, be said to be incarnations of Him. But this leads us nowhere. Rama, Krishna, etc. are called incarnations of God because we attribute divine qualities to them. Whether they actually lived or not does not affect the picture of them in man's mind.

—Gandhi, M.K., *Pathway to God*,
Navajivan Publishing House, 1971.

38

Advaitism and God

[In answer to a friend's question, Gandhiji wrote:]

I am an advaitist and yet I can support dvaitism (dualism). The world is changing every moment, and is therefore unreal, it has no permanent existence. But though it is constantly changing, it has a something about it which persists and it is therefore to that extent real. I have therefore no objection to calling it real and unreal, and thus being called an anekantavadi or a syaduadi. But my syadvada is not the syadvada of the learned, it is peculiarly my own. I cannot engage in a debate with them. It has been my experience that I am always true from my point of view, and am often wrong from the point of view of my honest critics. I know that we are both right from our respective points of view. And this knowledge saves me from attributing motives to my opponents or critics. The seven blind men who gave seven different descriptions of the elephant were all right from their respective points of view, and wrong from the point of view of one another, and right and wrong from the point of view of the man who knew the elephant. I very much like this doctrine of the manyness of reality. It is this doctrine that has taught me to judge a Mussulman from his own standpoint and a Christian from his. Formerly I used to resent the ignorance of my opponents. Today I can love them because I am gifted with the eye to see myself as others see me and vice versa. I want to take the whole world in the embrace of my love. My anekantavada is the result of the twin doctrine of satya and ahimsa.

I talk of God exactly as I believe Him to be. I believe Him to be creative as well as non-creative. This too is the result of my acceptance of the doctrine of the manyness of reality. From the platform of the Jains I prove the non- creative aspect of God, and from that of Ramanuja the creative aspect. As a matter of fact we are all thinking of the Unthinkable, describing the Indescribable, seeking to know the Unknown, and that is why our speech falters, is inadequate and even often contradictory. That is why the Vedas describe Brahman as 'not this', 'not this'. But if He or It is not this, He or It is.

If we exist, if our parents and their parents have existed, then it is proper to believe in the Parent of the whole creation. If He is not, we are nowhere. And that is why all of us with one voice call one God differently as Paramatma, Ishwara, Shiva, Vishnu, Rama, Allah, Khuda, Dada Hormuzda, Jehova, God, and an infinite variety of names. He is one and yet many; He is smaller than an atom, and bigger than the Himalayas. He is contained even in a drop of the ocean, and yet not even the seven seas can compass Him. Reason is powerless to know Him. He is beyond the reach or grasp of reason. But I need not labour the point. Faith is essential in this matter. My logic can make and unmake innumerable hypotheses. An atheist might floor me in a debate. But my faith runs so very much faster than my reason that I can challenge the whole world and say, 'God is, was and ever shall be.'

But those who want to deny His existence are at liberty to do so. He is merciful and compassionate. He is not an earthly king needing an army to make us accept His sway. He allows us freedom, and yet His compassion commands obedience to His will. But if any one of us disdain to bow to His will, He says: 'So be it. My sun will shine no less for thee, my clouds will rain no less for thee. I need not force thee to accept my sway.' Of such a God let the ignorant dispute the existence. I am one of the millions of wise men who believe in Him and am never tired of bowing to Him and singing His glory.

—Gandhi, M.K., *Young India*, 21 January 1926.

39

On Idol Worship

I am both an idolator and an iconoclast in what I conceive to be the true senses of the terms. I value the spirit behind idol-worship. It plays a most important part in the uplift of the human race. And I would like to possess the ability to defend with my life the thousands of holy temples which sanctify this land of ours.

I am an iconoclast in the sense that I break down the subtle form of idolatry in the shape of fanaticism that refuses to see any virtue in any other form of worshipping the Deity save one's own. This form of idolatry is more deadly for being more fine and evasive than the tangible and gross form of worship that identifies the Deity with a little bit of a stone or a golden image.

—Gandhi, M.K., *Young India*, 23 August 1924, p. 284.

Whether the temples should contain images or not is a matter of temperament and taste. I do not regard a Hindu or a Roman Catholic place of worship containing images as necessarily bad or superstitious, and a mosque or a Protestant place of worship as good or free of superstition merely because of their exclusion of images. A symbol such as a Cross or a book may easily become idolatrous, and therefore superstitious. And the worship of the image of

Child Krishna or Virgin Mary may become ennobling and free of all superstition. It depends upon the attitude of the heart of the worshipper. I think that idol-worship is part of human nature. We hanker after symbolism. Why should one be more composed in a church than elsewhere? Images are an aid to worship. No Hindu considers an image to be God. I do not consider idol-worship a sin.

—Gandhi, M.K., *Young India*,
5 November 1925, p. 378.

'If Hinduism became monotheistic,' suggested the Father, 'Christianity and Hinduism can serve India in co-operation.'

'I would love to see the co-operation happen', said Gandhiji. 'I have my own solution, but in the first instance, I dispute the description that Hindus believe in many gods and are idolators. I believe that I am a thorough Hindu but I never believe in many gods. Never even in my childhood did I hold that belief, and no one ever taught me to do so.'

'As for idol-worship, you cannot do without it in some form or other. Why does a Mussalman give his life for defending a mosque which he calls a house of God? And why does a Christian go to a church, and when he is required to take an oath he swears by the Bible? Not that I see any objection to it. And what is it if not idolatry to give untold riches for building mosques and tombs? And what do the Roman Catholics do when they kneel before Virgin Mary and before saints—quite imaginary figures in stone or painted on canvas or glass?'

'But', objected the Catholic Father, 'I keep my mother's photo and kiss it in veneration of her. But I do not worship it, nor do I worship saints. When I worship

God, I acknowledge Him as Creator and greater than any human being.'

'Even so, it is not the stone we worship, but it is God we worship in images of stone or metal however crude they may be.'

'But villagers worship stones as God.'

'No, I tell you they do not worship anything that is less than God. When you kneel before Virgin Mary and ask for her intercession, what do you do? You ask to establish contact with God through her. Even so a Hindu seeks to establish contact with God through a stone image. I can understand your asking for the Virgin's intercession. Why are Mussalmans filled with awe and exultation when they enter a mosque? Why, is not the whole universe a mosque? And what about the magnificent canopy of heaven that spreads over you ? Is it any less than a mosque? But I understand and sympathize with the Muslims. It is their way of approach to God. The Hindus have their own way of approach to the same Eternal Being. Our media of approach are different, but that does not make Him different.'

—Desai, Mahadev, *Harijan*, 13 March 1937, pp. 39–40.

Image-worship in the sense of investing one's ideal with a concrete shape is inherent in man's nature, and even valuable as an aid to devotion. Thus we worship an image when we offer homage to a book which we regard as holy or sacred. We worship an image when we visit a temple or a mosque with a feeling of sanctity or reverence. Nor do I see any harm in all this. On the contrary endowed as man is with a finite, limited understanding, he can hardly do otherwise.

The offering of vows and prayers for selfish ends, whether offered in churches, mosques, temples or before trees and shrines, is a thing not to be encouraged. Making a selfish request or offering of vows is not related to image worship as effect and cause. A personal selfish prayer is bad whether made before an image or an unseen God.

—Gandhi, M.K., *Young India*,
26 September 1929, p. 320.

40

Approach Temples in Faith

In the days of my youth I went to many temples with the faith and devotion with which my parents had fired me. But of late years I have not been visiting temples, and ever since I have been engaged in anti-untouchability work, I have refrained from going to temples unless they were open to every one called untouchable.

So what I saw this morning at the temple dawned upon me with the same newness with which it must have dawned upon so many avarna Hindus who must have gone to the temple after the Proclamation. In imagination my mind travelled back to the pre-historic centuries when temples began to convey the message of God in stone and metal. I saw quite clearly that the priest who was interpreting each figure in his own choice Hindi did not want to tell me that each of those figures was God. But without giving me that particular interpretation he made me realize that these temples were so many bridges between the Unseen, Invisible and Indefinable God and ourselves who are infinitesimal drops in the Infinite Ocean.

We the human family are not all philosophers. We are of the earth very earthy, and we are not satisfied with contemplating the Invisible God. Somehow or other we want something which we can touch, something which we can see, something before which we can kneel down. It does not matter whether it is a book, or an empty stone building, or a stone building inhabited by numerous figures.

A book will satisfy some, an empty building will satisfy some others, and many others will not be satisfied unless they see something inhabiting these empty buildings. Then I ask you to approach these temples not as if they represented a body of superstitions. If you will approach these temples with faith in them, you will know that each time you visit them you will come away from them purified, and with your faith more and more in the living God.

—Gandhi, M.K., *Harijan*, 23 January 1937.

41

The Spinning Wheel and God

I want to see the spinning wheel everywhere, because I see pauperism everywhere. Not until and unless we have fed and clothed the skeletons of India, will religion have any meaning for them.

They are living the cattle-life today, and we are responsible for it. The spinning wheel is therefore a penance for us. Religion is service of the helpless. God manifests Himself to us in the form of the helpless and the stricken. But we in spite of our forehead marks take no notice of them i.e. of God. God is and is not in the Vedas.

—Gandhi, M.K., *Young India*, 14 August 1924.

I think of the poor of India every time that I draw a thread on the wheel. The poor of India today have lost faith in God, more so than the middle classes or the rich. For a person suffering from the pangs of hunger, and desiring nothing but to fill his belly is his God. To him any one who gives him his bread is his Master. Through him he may even see God. To give alms to such persons, who are sound in all their limbs, is to debase oneself and them. What they need is some kind of occupation, and the occupation that will give employment to millions can only be hand-spinning.

I have described my spinning as a penance or sacrament. And, since I believe that where there is pure and active love for the poor there is God also, I see God in every thread that I draw on the spinning-wheel.

—Gandhi, M.K., *Young India*, 20 May 1926.

The spinning-wheel enables us to identify ourselves with cores. The millionaires imagine that money can bring them anything in the world. But it is not so. At any moment death might come and snuff them out... Losing one's life [...] is not the same thing as shedding 'self'. One has to learn to efface self or the ego voluntarily and as a sacrifice in order to find God. The spinning-wheel rules out exclusiveness. It stands for all inclusiveness. It stands for all including the poorest. It, therefore, requires us to be humble and to cast away pride completely.

—Gandhi, M.K., *Harijan*, 13 October 1946, p. 345.

Revival of the cottage industry, and not cottage industries, will remove the growing poverty. When once we have revived the one industry, all the other industries will follow... I would make the spinning-wheel the foundation on which to build a sound village life. I would make the wheel the centre round which all other activities will revolve.

—Gandhi, M.K., *Young India*, 21 May 1925, pp. 176–77.

I... claim for the Charkha the honour of being able to solve the problem of economic distress in a most natural, simple, inexpensive and business like manner... It is the symbol of the nation's prosperity and, therefore, freedom. It is a symbol not of commercial war but of commercial peace.

—Gandhi, M.K., *Young India*,
8 December 1921, p. 406.

I believe that no other path but that of non-violence will suit India. The symbol of that *dharma* for India is the spinning-wheel as it alone is the friend of the distressed and the giver of plenty for the poor. The law of love knows no bounds of space or time. My Swaraj, therefore, takes note of Bhangis, Dublas and the weakest of the weak, and except the spinning-wheel I know no other thing which befriends all these.

—Gandhi, M.K., *Young India*, 8 January 1925, p. 18.

He who reads the spirit of the Vedas sees God therein. He who clings to the letter of the Vedas is a vedia—a literalist. Narasinha Mehta does indeed sing the praise of the rosary, and the praise is well-merited where it is given. But the same Narasinha has sung:

> Of what avail is the *tilaka* and the *tulsi*, of what avail is the rosary and the muttering of the Name, what avail is the grammatical interpretation of the *Veda*, what avail is the mastery of the letters? All these are devices to fill the belly and nothing worth without their helping to a realization of the *Parabrahma*.

The Mussulman does count the beads of his tasbih, and the Christian of the rosary. But both would think themselves fallen from religion if their tasbih and rosary prevented them from running to the succour of one who, for instance, was lying stricken with a snake-bite.

Mere knowledge of the Vedas cannot make our Brahman as spiritual preceptors. If it did, Max Muller would have become one. The brahmana who has understood the religion of today will certainly give Vedic learning a secondary place and propagate the religion of the spinning wheel, relieve the hunger of the millions of his starving countrymen and only then, and not until then, lose himself in Vedic studies.

I have certainly regarded spinning superior to the practice of denominational religions. But that does not mean that the latter should be given up. I only mean that a dharma which has to be observed by the followers of all religions transcends them, and hence I say that a brahmana is a better brahmana, a Mussulman a better Mussulman, a Vaishnava a better Vaishnava, if he turns the wheel in the spirit of service.

If it was possible for me to turn the wheel in my bed, and if I felt that it would help me in concentrating my mind on God, I would certainly leave the rosary aside and turn the wheel. If I am strong enough to turn the wheel, and I have to make a choice between counting beads or turning the wheel, I would certainly decide in favour of the wheel, making it my rosary, so long as I found poverty and starvation stalking the land.

I do look forward to a time when even repeating the name of Rama will become a hindrance. When I have realized that Rama transcends even speech, I shall have no need to repeat the name. The spinning wheel, the rosary and the Ramanama are all the same to me.

They subserve the same end, they teach me the religion of service. I cannot practice ahitnsa without practising the religion of service, and I cannot find the truth without practising the religion of ahimsa. And there is no religion other than truth. Truth is Rama, Narayana, Ishwara, Khuda, Allah, God. As Narasinha says, 'The different shapes into which gold is beaten gives rise to different names and forms; but ultimately it is all gold.'

—Gandhi, M.K., *Young India*, 14 August 1924.

42

Krishna in the Gita of Karma

My Krishna has nothing to do with any historical person. I would refuse to bow my head to the Krishna who would kill because his pride is hurt, or the Krishna whom 'non-Hindus portray as a dissolute youth. I believe in Krishna of my imagination as a perfect incarnation, spotless in every sense of the word, the inspirer of the Gita and the inspirer of the lives of millions of human beings. But if it was proved to me that the Mahabharata is history in the same sense that modern historical books are, that every word of the Mahabharata is authentic and that the Krishna of the Mahabharata actually did some of the acts attributed to him, even at the risk of being banished from the Hindu fold, I should not hesitate to reject that Krishna as God incarnate. But to me, the Mahabharata is a profoundly religious book, largely allegorical, in no way meant to be a historical record. It is the description of the eternal duel going on within ourselves, given so vividly as to make us think for the time being, that the deeds described therein were actually done by the human beings. Nor do I regard the Mahabharata as we have it now as a faultless copy of the original. On the contrary I consider that it has undergone many emendations.

—Gandhi, M.K., *Young India*, 1 October 1925, p. 336.

Krishna in the Gita of Karma

[The following is a summary of a speech delivered by Gandhiji at Arsikere in Mysore State:]

We do not know what Shri Krishna's life means for us, we do not read the Gita, we make no attempt to teach it to our children. The Gita is such a transcendental book that men of every creed, age and clime may read it with respect, and find in it the principles of their respective religions.

If we thought of Krishna on every Janmashtami day and read the Gita and resolved to follow its teachings, we should not be in our present sorry plight. Shri Krishna served the people all his life, he was a real servant of the people. He could have led the hosts at Kurukshetra, but he preferred to be Arjuna's charioteer. His whole life was one unbroken Gita of karma.

He refused proud Duryodhana's sweets and preferred humble Vidura's spinach. As a child he was a cowherd and we still know him by the name of Gopala. But we, his worshippers, have neglected the cow today, the Adi-Karnatakas slaughter cows and eat beef, and our infants and invalids have to go without cow's milk.

Krishna knew no sleep or idleness. He kept sleepless vigil of the world, we his posterity have become indolent and forgotten the use of our hands. In the Bhagawadgita Lord Krishna has shown the path of bhakti—which means the path of karma. Lokamanya Tilak has shown that whether we desire to be bhaktas or jnanis, karma is the only way; but the karma should not be for self but for others.

Action for one's own self binds, action for the sake of others delivers from bondage. What can be the altruistic action which can be universally done, by Hindus, Mussulmans, Christians, by men, women and children?

I have tried to demonstrate that spinning alone is that sacrificial act, for that alone can make us do something in God's name, something for the poorest, something that can infuse activity in their idle limbs. Lord Krishna has also taught that to be a true bhakta we should make no difference between a brahmana and a scavenger. If that is true there can be no place for untouchability in Hinduism.

If you are still hugging that superstition you can cleanse yourself by getting rid of it on this the sacred day of Krishna's birth. He who swears by the Gita may know no distinction between Hindu and Mussulman, for Lord Krishna has declared that he who adores God in a true spirit by whatsoever name adores Him. The path of bhakti, karma, love as expounded in the Gita, leaves no room for the despising of man by man.

—Gandhi, M.K., *Young India*, 1 September 1927.

43

Ramanama

I know from correspondence with the students all over India, what wrecks they have become by having stuffed their brains with information derived from a cartload of books. Some have become unhinged, others have become lunatics, some have been leading a life of helpless impurity. My heart goes out to them when, they say that try as much as they might, they are what they are, because they cannot overpower the devil. 'Tell us,' they plaintively ask, 'how to get rid of the devil, how to get rid of the impurity that has seized us.' When I ask them to take Ramanama and kneel before God and seek His help, they come to me and say: 'We do not know where God is. We do not know what it is to pray.' That is the state to which they have been reduced...

A Tamil saying has always remained in my memory, and it means: 'God is the Help of the helpless.' If you would ask Him to help you, you would go to Him in all your nakedness, approach Him without reservations, also without fear of doubts as to how He can help a fallen being like you. He who has helped millions who have approached Him, is He going to desert you? He makes no exception whatsoever, and you will find that everyone of your prayers will be answered. The prayer of even the most impure will be answered. I am telling this out of my personal experience. I have gone through the purgatory. Seek first the Kingdom of Heaven and everything will be added unto you.

—Gandhi, M.K., *Young India*, 4 April 1929, p. 110.

But prayer is no mere exercise of words or of the ears, it is no mere repetition of empty formula. Any amount of repetition of Ramanama is futile, if it fails to stir the soul. It is better in prayer to have a heart without words, than words without a heart. It must be in clear response to the spirit which hungers for it. And even as a hungry man relishes a hearty meal, a hungry soul will relish a heartfelt prayer. And I am giving you a bit of my experience, and that of my companions, when I say that he who has experienced the magic of prayer may do without food for days together, but not a single moment without prayer. For without prayer there is no inward peace.

There is no doubt that Ramanama is the surest aid. If recited from the heart, it charms away every evil thought; and evil thought gone, no corresponding action is possible. The outward helps are all useless if, the mind is weak. They are superfluous if the mind is pure. This must not be taken to mean that a pure-minded man can take all the liberties and still keep safe. Such a man simply will not take any liberties with himself. His whole life will be an infallible testimony to the inward purity. The *Gita* truly says that mind makes the man and unmakes him. Milton paraphrases the same thought when he says: 'The mind is its own place, and in itself can make a Heaven of Hell, a Hell of Heaven.'

—Gandhi, M.K., *Young India*, 23 January 1930, p. 25.

44

Ramadhun

An Arya Samajist writes:

> 'How can the Rama whom you believe to be immortal, be Rama, the son of Dasharatha and the husband of Sita? I often attend your prayer gathering with this dilemma always confronting me and because of it. I am unable to join in the Ramadhun. This hurts me. for you are right when you say that all should take part in it. Cannot you make the Ramadhun such that all can join in the recital ?'

I have already explained what I mean by *all*. It applies to all those who can join in it from the heart and recite it in tune. The others should remain silent. But this is a small matter. The important question is as to how Rama, the son of Dasharatha, can be deemed immortal. This question was raised by Saint Tulsidas himself and answered by him. The answer cannot in reality be reasoned out. It does not lend itself to intellectual satisfaction. It is a matter of heart speaking to heart. I worshipped Rama as Sita's husband in the first instance, but as my knowledge and experience of Him grew, my Rama became immortal and omnipresent. This does not mean that Rama ceased to be Sita's husband.

But the meaning of Sita's husband expanded with the vision of Rama. This is how the world evolves. Rama cannot become omnipresent for the man who regards him merely as the son of Dasharatha. But for the believer in Rama as God, the father of the omnipresent, Rama also becomes omnipresent—the father and son become one. It may be said that this is all a matter of imagination. 'To each man according to his faith,' is all that I can say. If all religions are one at source, we have to synthesize them. Today, they are looked upon as separate and that is why we kill each other. When we are tired of religion, we become atheists and then, apart from the little self, nothing, not even God, exists. But when we acquire true understanding, the little self perishes and God becomes all in all. Rama, then, is and is not the son of Dasharatha, the husband of Sita, the brother of Bharata and Lakshmana and yet is God, the unborn and eternal. All honour, then, to those who not believing in Rama as the son of Dasharatha still come to join in the collective prayers. This matter of Rama is one which transcends reason. I have merely tried to give to the reader my belief for what it is worth.

—Gandhi, M.K., *Harijan*, 22 September 1946, p. 32.

45

The Remedy of Ramanama

In *Ayurveda*, there is ample testimony to the efficacy of Ramanama as a cure for all disease. Nature Cure occupies the place of honour and in it Ramanama is the most important. When Charaka, Vagbhata and other giants of medicine in ancient India wrote, the popular name for God was not Rama but Vishnu. I myself have been a devotee of Tulsidas from my childhood and have, therefore, always worshipped God as Rama. But I know that if beginning with *Omkar*, one goes through the entire gamut of God's names current in all climes, all countries and all languages, the result is the same. He and His Law are one. To observe His Law is, therefore, the best form of worship. A man who becomes one with the Law does not stand in need of vocal recitation of the name. In other words, an individual with whom contemplation on God has become as natural as breathing is so filled with God's spirit that knowledge or observance of the Law becomes second nature, as it were, with him. Such a one needs no other treatment.

The question, then, arises as to why, in spite of having this prince of remedies at hand, we know so little about it; and why even those who know, do not remember Him or remember Him only by lip service, not from the heart.

Parrot-like repetition of God's name signifies failure to recognize Him as the panacea for all ills.

How can they? This sovereign remedy is not administered by doctors, *vaidyas*, *hakims* or any other medicinal practitioners. These have no faith in it. If they were to admit that the spring of the Holy Ganges could be found in every home, their very occupation or means of livelihood would go. Therefore, they must perforce rely on their powders and potions as infallible remedies. Not only do these provide bread for the doctor, but the patient, too, seems to feel immediate relief. If a medical practitioner can get a few persons to say: 'So and so gave me a powder and I was cured,' his business is established.

Nor, it must be borne in mind, would it really be of any use for doctors to prescribe God's name to patients unless they themselves were conscious of its miraculous powers. Ramanama is no copybook maxim. It is something, that has to be realized through experience. One who has had personal experience alone can prescribe it, not any other.

The *Vaidyaraj* has copied out for me four verses. Out of these, Charaka's is the simplest and most apt.

It means that if one were to obtain mastery over even one out of the thousand names of Vishnu, all ailments would vanish:

विष्णु सहस्रमूर्धानं चराचरपतिं विभुम् ।
स्तुवन् नामसहस्रेण ज्वरान् सर्वान् व्यपोहति ॥

—Gandhi, M.K., *Harijan*, 24 March 1936.

46

Ramarajya

By Ramrajya I do not mean Hindu Raj. I mean by Ramarajya Divine Raj, the Kingdom of God. For me Rama and Rahim are one and the same deity. I acknowledge no other God but the one God of truth and righteousness.

Whether Rama of my imagination ever lived or not on this earth, the ancient ideal of Ramarajya is undoubtedly one of true democracy in which the meanest citizen could be sure of swift justice without an elaborate and costly procedure. Even the dog is described by the poet to have received justice under Ramarajya.

—Gandhi, M.K., *Young India*,
19 September 1929, p. 305.

The rajya of my dream ensures equal rights alike of prince and pauper.

—Gandhi, M.K., *Amrita Bazar Patrika*, 4 August 1934.

By political independence I do not mean an imitation to the British House of commons, or the soviet rule of Russia or the Fascist rule of Italy or the Nazi rule of Germany. They have systems suited to their genius. We must have ours suited to ours. What that can be is more than I can tell. I have described it as Ramarajya i.e., sovereignty of the people based on pure moral authority.

—Gandhi, M.K., *Harijan*, 2 January 1937, p. 374.

Friends have repeatedly challenged me to define independence. At the risk of repetition, I must say that independence of my dream means Ramarajya i.e., the Kingdom of God on earth. I do not know it will be like in Heaven. I have no desire to know the distant scene. If the present is attractive enough, the future cannot be very unlike.

My conception of Ramarajya excludes the replacement of the British army by a national army of occupation. A country that is governed by even its national army can never be morally free and, therefore, its so-called weakest member can never rise to his fullest moral height.

—Gandhi, M.K., *Harijan*, 5 May 1946, p. 116.

There can be no Ramarajya in the present state of iniquitous inequalities in which a few roll in riches and the masses do not get even enough to eat [...] my opposition to the Socialists and other consists in attacking violence as a means of effecting any lasting reform.

—Gandhi, M.K., *Harijan*, 1 June 1947, p. 172.

I compare nirvana to Ramarajya or the Kingdom of Heaven on earth... The withdrawal of British power does not mean Ramarajya. How can it happen when we have all along been nursing violence in our hearts under the garb of non-violence?

—Gandhi, M.K., *Harijan*, 3 August 1947, p. 262.

If you want to see God in the form of Ramarajya, the first requisite is self-introspection. You have to magnify your own faults a thousand fold and shut your eyes to the faults of your neighbours. That is the only way to real progress.

—Gandhi, M.K., *Harijan*, 26 October 1947, p. 387.

My Hinduism teaches me to respect all religions. In this lies the secret of Ramarajya.

—Gandhi, M.K., *Harijan*, 19 October 1947, p. 378.

Truth
. . . .

47

What Is Truth?

A difficult question, but I have solved it for myself by saying that it is what the voice within tells you. How, then, you ask, different people think of different and contrary truths? Well, seeing that the human mind works through innumerable media and that the evolution of the human mind is not the same for all, it follows that what may be truth for one may be untruth for another, and hence those who have made these experiments have come to the conclusion that there are certain conditions to be observed in making those experiments. Just as for conducting scientific experiments there is an indispensable scientific course of instruction, in the same way strict preliminary discipline is necessary to qualify a person to make experiments in the spiritual realm. Everyone should, therefore, realize his limitations before he speaks of his inner voice. Therefore we have the belief based upon experience, that those who would make individual search after truth as God, must go through several vows, as for instance, the vow of truth, the vow of brahmacharya (purity)—for you cannot possibly divide your love for Truth and God with anything else— the vow of non-violence, of poverty and non-possession. Unless you impose on yourselves the five vows you may not embark on the experiment at all. There are several other conditions prescribed, but I must not take you through all of them. Suffice it to say that those who have made these experiments know that it is not proper for everyone to claim to hear the voice of conscience, and it is because we have at the present moment everybody claiming the right of conscience without going through any discipline whatsoever and there is so much untruth being delivered to a bewildered world, all that I can, in true humility, present to you is that truth is not to be found by anybody who has not got an abundant sense of humility.

For me truth is the sovereign principle, which includes numerous other principles. This truth is not only truthfulness in word, but truthfulness in thought also, and not only the relative truth of our conception, but the Absolute Truth, the Eternal Principle, that is God. There are innumerable definitions of God, because His manifestations are innumerable. They overwhelm me with wonder and awe and for a moment stun me. But I worship God as Truth only. I have not yet found Him, but I am seeking after Him. I am prepared to sacrifice the things dearest to me in pursuit of this quest. Even if the sacrifice demanded be my very life, I hope I may be prepared to give it. But as long as I have not realized this Absolute Truth, so long must I hold by the relative truth as I have conceived it. That relative truth must, meanwhile, be my beacon, my shield and buckler. Though this path is strait and narrow and sharp as the razor's edge, for me it has been the quickest and easiest. Even my Himalayan blunders have seemed trifling to me because I have kept strictly to this path. For the path has saved me from coming to grief, and I have gone forward according to my light. Often in

What Is Truth? ■ 189

my progress I have had faint glimpses of the Absolute Truth, God, and daily the conviction is growing upon me that He alone is real and all else is unreal... The further conviction has been growing upon me that whatever is possible for me is possible even for a child, and I have found sound reasons for saying so. The instruments for the quest of Truth are as simple as they are difficult. They may appear quite impossible to an arrogant person, and quite possible to an innocent child.

The seeker after Truth should be humbler than the dust. The world crushes the dust under its feet, but the seeker after Truth should so humble himself that even the dust could crush him. Only then, and not till then, will he have a glimpse of Truth. Truth is like a vast tree, which yields more and more fruit the more you nurture it. The deeper the search in the mine of truth the richer the discovery of the gems buried there, in the shape of openings for an even greater variety of service. In the march towards Truth, anger, selfishness, hatred, etc., naturally give way, for otherwise Truth would be impossible to attain. A man who is swayed by passions may have good enough intentions, may be truthful in word, but he will never find the Truth. A successful search for Truth means complete deliverance from the dual throng such as of love and hate, happiness and misery. I think it is wrong to expect certainties in this world, where all else but God that is Truth is an uncertainty. All that appears and happens about and around is uncertain, transient. But there is a Supreme Being hidden therein as a Certainty, and one would be blessed if one could catch a glimpse of that certainty and hitch one's wagon to it. The quest for that

Truth is the summum bonum of life. To see the universal and all-pervading spirit of Truth face to face one must be able to love the meanest of creation as oneself. And a man who aspires after that cannot afford to keep out of any field of life. That is why my devotion to Truth has drawn me into the field of politics; and I can say without the slightest hesitation, and yet in all humility, that those who say that religion has nothing to do with politics do not know what religion means. My uniform experience has convinced me that there is no other God than Truth... The little fleeting glimpses... that I have been able to have of Truth can hardly convey an idea of the indescribable luster of Truth, a million times more intense than that of the sun we daily see with our eyes.

In fact, what I have caught is only the faintest gleam of that mighty effulgence. But this much I can say with assurance, as a result of all my experiments, that a perfect vision of Truth can only follow a complete realization of ahimsa. Truth resides in every human heart, and one has to search for it there, and to be guided by truth as one sees it. But no one has a right to coerce others to act according to his own view of truth. If you would swim on the bosom of the ocean of Truth you must reduce yourself to a zero. Further than this I cannot go along this fascinating path.

—Gandhi, M.K., *Young India*, 31 December 1931.

48

The Ultimate Truth

To me God is Truth and Love: God is ethics and morality; God is fearlessness. God is the source of Light and Life and yet He is above and beyond all these. God is conscience. He is even the atheism of the atheist. For in His boundless love God permits the atheist to live. He is the searcher of hearts: He transcends speech and reason. He knows us and our hearts better than we do ourselves. He does not take us at our word for He knows that we often do not mean it, some knowingly and others unknowingly. He is a personal God to those who need His personal presence. He is embodied to those who need His touch. He is the purest essence. He simply *is* to those who have faith. He is all things to all men... He is in us and yet above and beyond us. One may banish the word 'God' from the Congress but one has no power to banish the Thing itself. What is a solemn affirmation, if it is not the same thing as in the name of God? And surely conscience is but a poor and laborious paraphrase of the simple combination of three letters called God. He cannot cease to be because hideous immoralities or inhuman brutalities are committed in His name. He is long suffering. He is patient but He is also terrible. He is the most exacting personage in the world and the world to come. He metes out the same measure to us as we mete out to our neighbours—men and brutes. With Him ignorance is no excuse. And withal He is ever forgiving for He always gives us the chance to repent. He is the greatest democrat the world knows, for He leaves us 'unfettered' to make our own choice between evil and good. He is the greatest tyrant ever known, for He often dashes the cup from our lips and under cover of free will leaves us a margin-so wholly inadequate as to provide only mirth for Himself at our expense. Therefore it is that Hinduism calls it all His sport—Lila, or calls it all an illusion—Maya. We are not, He alone Is. And if we will be, we must eternally sing His praise and do His will. Let us dance to the tune of His bansi—flute, and all would be well.

—Gandhi, M.K., 'My Crime', *Young India*,
5 March 1925, Vol. 7, No. 10, p. 81.

God is Truth, but God is many other things also. That is why I say Truth is God... Only remember that Truth is not one of the many qualities that we name. It is the living embodiment of God, it is the only Life, and I identify Truth with the fullest life, and that is how it becomes a concrete thing, for God is His whole creation, the whole Existence, and service of all that exists-Truth-is service of God.

I have not seen Him, neither have I known Him. I have made the world's faith in God my own and as my faith is ineffaceable, I regard that faith as amounting to experience. However, as it may be said that to describe faith as experience is to tamper with truth, it may perhaps be more correct to say that I have no word for characterizing my belief in God.

—Gandhi, M.K., *The Story of My Experiments with Truth*, Mahadev Desai (trans.), Navajivan Publishing House, 1948, p. 341.

I am surer of His existence than of the fact that you and I are sitting in this room. Then I can also testify that I may live without air and water but not without Him. You may pluck out my eyes, but that cannot kill me. You may chop off my nose, but that will not kill me. But blast my belief in God, and I am dead.

—Gandhi, M.K., *Harijan*, 14 May 1938, pp. 109.

49

The Power of Truth

'You have asked me why I consider that God is Truth. In my early youth I was taught to repeat what in Hindu scriptures are known as one thousand names of God. But these one thousand names of God were by no means exhaustive. We believe—and I think it is the truth—that God has as many names as there are creatures and, therefore, we also say that God is nameless and since God has many forms we also consider Him formless, and since He speaks to us through many tongues we consider Him to be speechless and so on. And so when I came to study Islam I found that Islam too had many names for God. I would say with those who say God is Love, God is Love. But deep down in me I used to say that though God may be love, God is Truth, above all. If it is possible for the human tongue to give the fullest description of God, I have come to the conclusion that for myself, God is Truth. But two years ago I went a step further and said that Truth is God. You will see the fine distinction between the two statements, viz. that God is Truth and Truth is God. And I came to that conclusion after a continuous and relentless search after Truth which began nearly fifty years ago. I then found that the nearest approach to Truth was through love. But I also found that love has many meanings in the English language at least and that human love in the sense of passion could become a degrading thing also. I found too that love in the sense of ahimsa had only a limited number of votaries in the world. But I never found a double meaning in connection with truth and even atheists had not demurred to the necessity or power of truth. But in their passion for discovering truth the atheists have not hesitated to deny the very existence of God—from their own point of view rightly. And it was because of this reasoning that I saw that rather than say that God is Truth I should say that Truth is God... There are thus a number of difficulties in the way, no matter how you describe God. But the human mind is a limited thing, and you have to labour under limitations when you think of a being or entity who is beyond the power of man to grasp.'

—Gandhi, M.K., 'Truth and God', *Young India*, Vol. 13, No. 53, 31 December 1931, pp. 427–28.

50

Truth and Love

The Force of love is the same as the force of the soul or truth. We have evidence of its working at every step. The universe would disappear without the existence of that force...

Thousands, indeed tens of thousands, depend for their existence on a very active working of this force. Little quarrels of millions of families in their daily lives disappear before the exercise of this force. Hundreds of nations live in peace. History does not and cannot take note of this fact. History is really a record of every interruption of the even working of the force of love or of the soul. Two brothers quarrel; one of them repents and reawakens the love that was lying dormant in him; the two again begin to live in peace; nobody takes note of this. But if the two brothers, through the intervention of solicitors or some other reason, take up arms or go to law-which is another form of the exhibition of brute force-their doings would be immediately noticed in the Press, they would be the talk of their neighbours and would probably go down to history. And what is true of families and communities is true of nations. There is no reason to believe that there is one law for families and another for nations. History, then, is a record of an interruption of the course of nature.

Soul force, being natural, is not noted in history.

—Gandhi, M.K., *Hind Swaraj or Indian Home Rule*,
Navajivan Publishing House, Ahmedabad, 1910.

Scientists tell us that, without the presence of the cohesive force amongst the atoms that comprise this globe of ours—it would crumble to pieces and we would cease to exist; and even as there is cohesive force in blind matter, so must there be in all things animate, and the name for that cohesive force among animate beings is love. We notice it between father and son, between brother and sister, friend and friend. But we have to learn to use that force among all that lives, and in the use of it consists our knowledge of God. Where there is love there is love there is life; hatred leads to destruction.

—Gandhi, M.K., 'Mr Gandhi's Speech', *Young India*,
Vol. 2, No. 18, 5 May 1920, pp. 6–7.

'I believe that the sum total of the energy of mankind is not to bring us down but to lift us up, and that is the result of the definite, if unconscious, working of the law of love. The fact that mankind persists shows that the cohesive force is greater than the disruptive force, centripetal force greater than centrifugal.'

—Quoted in Desai, Mahadev 'London Letter:
As We Were', *Young India*, Vol. 13, No. 46,
12 November 1931, pp. 351–52.

I have found that life persists in the midst of destruction and, therefore, there must be a higher law than that of destruction. Only under that law would a well-ordered society be intelligible and life worth living. And if that is the law of life, we have to work it out in daily life. Wherever there are jars, wherever you are confronted with an opponent, conquer him with love. In this crude manner, I have worked it out in my life. That does not mean that all my difficulties are solved. Only, I have found that this law of love has answered as the law of destruction has never done.

—Gandhi, M.K., 'From S.S. Rajputana', *Young India*, Vol. 13, No. 40, 1 October 1931, p. 286.

If love or non-violence be not the law of our being [...] there is no escape from a periodical recrudescence of war, each succeeding one outdoing the preceding one in ferocity... All the teachers that ever lived have preached that law with more or less vigour. If Love was not the law of life, life would not have persisted in the midst of death... Life is a perpetual triumph over the grave. If there is a fundamental distinction between man and beast, it is the former's progressive recognition of the law and its application in practice to his own personal life. All the saints of the world, ancient and modern, were each according to his light and capacity a living illustration of that supreme Law of our being. That the brute in us seems so often to gain an easy triumph is true enough. That, however, does not disprove the law. It shows the difficulty of practice. How should it be otherwise with a law which is as high as truth itself? When the practice of the law becomes universal, God will reign on earth as He does in Heaven. I need not be reminded that earth and Heaven are in us. We know the earth, we are strangers to the Heaven are in us. If it is allowed that for some the practice of love is possible, it is arrogance not to allow even the possibility of its practice in all the others. Not very remote ancestors of ours indulged in cannibalism and many other practice which we would today call loathsome. No doubt in those days too there were Dick Sheppard's who must have been laughed at and possibly pilloried for preaching the (to them) strange doctrine of refusing to eat fellow-men.

—Gandhi, M.K., 'The Law of Our Being', *Harijan*, 5 September 1936, Vol. 4, No. 30, p. 260.

History is a record of perpetual wars, but we are trying to make new history, and I say this as I represent the national mind so far as non-violence is concerned. I have reasoned out the doctrine of the sword, I have worked out its possibilities and come to the conclusion that men's destiny is to replace the law of the jungle with the law of conscious love.

—Desai, Mahadev 'Weekly Letter: A Herculean Task', *Harijan*, 03 July 1937, Vol. 5, No. 21, p. 165.

51
Truth and Beauty

'...There are two aspects of things—the outward and the inward... The outward has no meaning except in so far as it helps the inward. All true Art is thus an expression of the soul. The outward forms have value only in so far as they are the expression of the inner spirit of man... I know that many call themselves artists, and are recognized as such, and yet in their works there is absolutely no trace of the soul's upward urge and unrest.

'All true Art must help the soul to realize its inner self. In my own case, I find that I can do entirely without external forms in my soul's realization. I can claim, therefore, that there is truly efficient Art in my life, though you might not see what you call works of Art about me. My room may have blank walls; and I may even dispense with the roof, so that I may gaze out at the starry heavens overhead that stretch in an unending expanse. What conscious Art of man can give me the panoramic scenes that open out before me, when I look up to the sky above with all its shining stars? This, however, does not mean that I refuse to accept the value of productions of Art, generally accepted as such, but only that I personally feel how inadequate these are compared with the eternal symbols of beauty in Nature. These productions of man's

Art have their value only in so far as they help the soul onward towards self-realization.'

'Truth [...] is the first thing to be sought for, and Beauty and Goodness will then be added unto you. Jesus was, to my mind, a supreme artist because he saw and expressed Truth; and so was Muhammad, the Koran being, the most perfect composition in all Arabic literature—at any rate, that is what scholars say. It is because both of them strove first for Truth that the grace of expression naturally came in and yet neither Jesus not Muhammad wrote on Art. That is the Truth and Beauty I crave for, live for, and would die for.'

'To a true artist only that face is beautiful which, quite apart from its exterior, shines with the Truth within the soul. There is [...] no Beauty apart from Truth. On the other hand, Truth may manifest itself in forms, which may not be outwardly beautiful at all. Socrates, we are told, was the most truthful man of his time, and yet his features are said to have been the ugliest in Greece. To my mind he was beautiful, because all his life was a striving after Truth, and you may remember that his outward form did not prevent Phidias from appreciating the beauty of Truth in him, though as an artist he was accustomed to see Beauty in outward forms also.'

—Quoted in Desai, Mahadev, 'A Morning with Gandhiji', *Young India*, 13 November 1924, Vol. 6, No. 46, pp. 377–8.

'...[H]ere too, just as elsewhere, I must think in terms of the millions. And to the millions we cannot give that training to acquire a perception of Beauty in such a way as to see Truth in it. Show them Truth first and they will see Beauty afterwards... Whatever can be useful to those starving millions is beautiful to my mind. Let us give today first the vital things of life and all the graces and ornaments of life will follow.'

'I see and find Beauty in Truth or through Truth. All Truths, not merely true ideas, but truthful faces, truthful pictures or songs are highly beautiful. People generally fail to see Beauty in Truth, the ordinary man runs away from it and becomes blind to the beauty in it. Whenever men begin to see Beauty in Truth, then true Art will arise.'

—Gandhi, M.K., 'A Morning with Gandhiji', *Young India*, 20 November 1924, Vol. 6, No. 47, p. 386.

'...Truth and Untruth often co-exist; good and evil are often found together. In an artist also not seldom [do] the right perception of things and the wrong co-exist. Truly beautiful creations come when right perception is at work. If these monuments are rare in life, they are also rare in Art.'

'...[T]hese beauties ["a sunset or a crescent moon that shines amid the stars at night"] are truthful, inasmuch as they make me think of the Creator at the back of them. How else could these be beautiful, but for the Truth that is in the centre of creation? When I admire the wonder of a sunset or the beauty of the moon, my soul expands in worship of the Creator. I try to see Him and His mercies in all these creations. But even the sunsets and sunrises would be mere hindrances if they did not help me to think of the soul is a delusion and a snare; even like the body, which often does hinder you in the path of salvation.'

—Quoted in Desai, Mahadev, 'A Morning with Gandhiji', *Young India*, 13 November 1924, Vol. 6, No. 46, pp. 377–78.

'Why can't you see the beauty of colour in vegetables? And then, there is beauty in the speckless sky. But no, you want the colours of the rainbow, which is a mere optical illusion. We have been taught to believe that what is beautiful need not be useful and what is useful cannot be beautiful. I want to show that what is useful can also be beautiful.'

—Gandhi, M.K., 'Weekly letters: What is Beauty?', *Harijan*, 7 April 1946, Vol. 10, No. 9, p. 67.

I love music and all the other arts, but I do not attach such value to them as is generally done. I cannot, for example, recognize the value of those activities which require technical knowledge for their understanding. Life is greater than all art. I would go even further and declare that the man whose life comes nearest to perfection is the greatest artist; for what is art without the sure foundation and framework of a noble life?

—Fülöp-Miller, René, *Lenin and Gandhi*, F.S. Flint and D.F. Tait (trans.), G.P. Putnam's Sons, London, p. 210.

'We have somehow accustomed ourselves to the belief that art is independent of the purity of private life. I can say with all the experience at my command that nothing could be more untrue. As I am nearing the end of my earthly life, I can say that purity of life, is the highest and truest art. The art of producing good music from a cultivated voice can be achieved by many, but the art of producing that music from the harmony of a pure life is achieved very rarely.'

—'Gandhiji's Health', *Harijan*, 19 February 1938, Vol. 6, No. 2, p. 10.

52

My Mission

I do not consider myself worthy to be mentioned in the same breath with the race of prophets. I am a humble seeker after truth. I am impatient to realize myself, to attain *Moksha* in this very existence. My national service is part of my training for freeing my soul from the bondage of flesh. Thus considered, my service may be regarded as purely selfish. I have no desire for the perishable kingdom of earth. I am striving for the Kingdom of Heaven which is moksha. To attain my end it is not necessary for me to seek the shelter of a cave. I carry one about me, if I would but know it. A cave-dweller can build castles in the air whereas a dweller in a palace like Janak has no castles to build. The cave-dweller who hovers round the world on the wings of thought has no peace. A Janak though living in the midst of 'pomp and circumstance' may have peace that passeth understanding. For me the road to salvation lies through incessant toil in the service of my country and therethrough of humanity. I want to identify myself with everything that lives. In the language of the Gita I want to live at peace with both friend and foe. Though therefore a Mussulman or a Christian or a Hindu may despise me and hate me. I want to love him and serve him even as I would love my wife or son though they hate me. So my patriotism is for me a stage in my journey to the land of eternal freedom and peace. Thus it will be seen that for me there are no politics devoid of religion. They subserve religion. Politics bereft of religion are a death-trap because they kill the soul.

—Gandhi, M.K., 'My Mission', *Young India*, Vol. 6, No. 14, 3 April 1924, p. 113.

I feel that India's mission is different from that of the others. India if fitted of the religious supremacy of the world. There is no parallel in the world for the process of purification that this country has voluntarily undergone. India is less in need of steel weapons, it has fought with divine weapons; it can still do so. Other nations have been votaries of brute force. The terrible war going on in Europe furnishes a forcible illustration of the truth. India can win all by soul force.

—Gandhi, M.K., *Speeches and Writings of M.K. Gandhi*, G.A. Natesan and Company, 1922, p. 405.

That Indians are not a nation of cowards is proved by the personal bravery and daring of her martial races, whether Hindus, Mussalman, Sikh or Gurkha. My point is that the spirit of fighting is foreign to India's soil and that probably she has a higher part to play in the evolution of the world. Time alone can show what is to be her destiny.

—Gandhi, M.K., 'Our Shortcomings', *Young India*, Vol. 3, No. 25, 22 June 1921, p. 199.

India's destiny lies not along the bloody way of the West, of which she shows signs of tiredness, but along the bloodless way of peace that comes from a simple and godly life. India is in danger of losing her soul. She cannot lose it and live. She must not therefore lazily and helplessly say, 'I cannot escape the onrush from the West'. She must be strong enough to resist it for her own sake and that of the world.

—Gandhi, M.K., 'The Same Old Argument', *Young India*, 7 October 1926, Vol. 8, No. 40, 7 October 1926, p. 348.

India has an unbroken tradition of non-violence from times immemorial. But at no time in her ancient history, as far as I know, has it had complete non-violence in action pervading the whole land. Nevertheless, it is my unshakable belief that her destiny is to deliver the message of non-violence to mankind. It may take ages to come to fruition. But so far as I judge, no other country will precede her in the fulfillment of that mission.

—Gandhi, M.K., *Harijan*, 12 October 1935, p. 276.

On India rests the burden of pointing the way to all the exploited races of the earth. She won't be able to bear that burden today if non-violence does not permeate her more than [it does] today. I have been trying to fit ourselves for that mission by giving a wider bend to our struggle. India will become a torch-bearer to the oppressed and exploited races only if she can vindicate the principle of non-violence in her own case, not jettison it as soon as independence of foreign control is achieved.

—Gandhi, M.K., *Harijan*, 19 May 1946, p. 134.